THE DAWNS OF LIFE

An Exploration Into The Origins & Development Of Existence

Dictation from The Great White Brotherhood

Bob Sanders

DISCLAIMERS

This is a free eBook. You are free to give it away (in unmodified form) to whomever you wish. If you have paid for this eBook you should request or seek an immediate refund.

The author has made every effort to ensure that the accuracy of the information within this book was correct at time of publication. The author does not assume and hereby disclaims any liability to any party for any loss, damage, or disruption caused by errors or omissions, whether such errors or omissions result from accident, negligence, or any other cause.

COPYRIGHT

This book was authored by Bob Sanders and dictated to him from The Great White Brotherhood by clairaudience, or as some people call "channelling". It is free for everyone to read and share unmodified for spiritual advancement.

Please share this book unmodified with anyone and anywhere you can to help spread the messages it contains.

For more information please visit the following internet sites:

https://www.thegreatwhitebrotherhood.org

https://www.thestairwaytofreedom.org

https://www.youtube.com/channel/UC2UDv0r4mtNPEWbve5YHDeg/

First edition – May 2018

Cover artwork by Paul Saunders

Author – Bob Sanders

ISBN: 9781982956806
Imprint: Independently published

FOREWORD

We are going to describe in this volume another aspect of life which will be quite unlike anything that we have so far mentioned. And yet it will actually take us a step closer to the reality of life.

In the previous books we have mentioned at some length the creation of life in all the various dimensions, the way that life in general and human life in particular has been created, partly by God, partly by Archangels and partly through imagination.

We hope that you have read these books and all the various essays we have also given so that you have a firm foundation of the way life was created long ages ago and has progressed until the present time.

All that information was given because that is the way that life is viewed both by people incarnate and also by most people discarnate.

Due to the collective wisdom and understanding it has created a form of reality in the so called physical realms and also in the spiritual realms.

But, we wish to tell you – and hope you won't be offended – but nothing that we mentioned before is actually true.

It is all imagination that people accept as true.

Certainly, all that we said in the three first books and the many essays and information that we have given you, you could repeat to others and no one would disagree with you because it is collective wisdom – often taken on beyond what is generally known – and appears true.

To a certain extent it is true, but the problem with life is that it is endless. Each time we think that we have a firm understanding concerning a certain portion of life, we find, either to our joy or our dismay that what we know, or think we know, is just one aspect and, if we have the skill, we can open a door into a whole new realm hitherto unknown.

Perhaps we could use simple analogy. Imagine that people studied animals on Earth but just on land until they knew absolutely everything that there was to be known about land-based animals.

But then they discovered that there were creatures that flew in the skies that no one had noticed; birds, butterflies etc.

So, the searches would have to start all over again and study flying creatures.

Then, once they had learned all that there was to know about land-based creatures and flying creatures, someone informed them that, in the seas, more life existed.

We realize that this is a rather feeble analogy but we want to make the point that life can be quite complicated or complex and all that we know so far about life is not necessarily all that there is to know.

Further, and to make the story even more difficult to accept, is that all is illusion but presented as real.

So long as we just accept what we have presented to you so far, which is in its realm true, as all there is, there is no problem.

But, if we are informed that there is life outside of what we know and that this new life actually replaces the life you thought you knew, it starts to create problems.

So, we wish for you clearly to understand that all that we have told you is true so long as you stay within the confines of life in all the different dimensions, inter-dimensions and areas of existence that are known to man.

But there are creations of life piled one on top of another rather like building blocks – or Russian Dolls would perhaps be a better image – the point being that once we learn about a new life we realize that the previous one was just illusion.

We hope and expect that this new version of life would be true but, of course, it will fade to illusion as we uncover yet another aspect of life.

But we can only discover one new reality at a time so this book will venture out from the known areas of life as has been explained and will explore the next level.

No doubt some of you will not be able, immediately, to assimilate the knowledge we will impart, but it is important to explain as much as we can about the endless realities of life, so we give this information and leave acceptance or rejection in your hands.

Our job is to give information. Your job is to read it and accept what you can. We wish you good fortune as, together, we explore the world we wish to reveal.

CHAPTER 1

A RESUME OF LIFE

Imagine if it were possible to look around you wherever you are at this moment and, instead of seeing the things that in all probability you have seen many times before, it all looked different. For instance, some of you might be in what is called a living room. Others might be in a bedroom. No matter where you are, what would your reaction be if everything suddenly looked different, unrecognisable?

Would you be frightened? Or would you be curious?

Would you do all in your power to make the new world go away or would you have the desire to explore this new vista?

We asked these questions for a reason.

As we have stated in other publications, to a large extent we create with our imagination the world that we see around us.

We tend – most of us – to want that world to be stable, solid, familiar, friendly, reassuring. So, with our imaginations we do our best to create that sort of environment and we just accept that as life. Of course, life also, from time to time, sends us challenges that we do our best to resolve and then return to our familiar world, created by us individually and collectively.

Now, as we move into what is called Ascension, which is the result of spiritual power shining on us so, sometimes we get glimpses into other realities, the spirit world or the etheric planes. We do this with our mind. The physical body tends to stay in our 3D world.

Some, there are, that deliberately train to contact the invisible realms and learn to contact discarnate beings. These spiritual realms, we have stated, are many and there are a number of different realms that one can explore but it is nearly always done with just our spiritual bodies.

Our physical body remains on terra-firma, as it is called.

We have also explained that the physical body is, itself, an aspect of spirituality and, when we can realize this, it is possible to make it function rather as we can use our other spiritual parts. For instance, teleportation is possible to learn which is the ability to move instantly from one place to another. Very few people bother to learn to do this but it is possible.

It is also possible to see physical objects whilst blindfolded – a skill that some children are now being trained to do.

On the subject of teleportation, we have also explained to you that many alien visitors to our realms create crafts (UFOs) that are actually living objects and can teleport around our world.

So, the point that we are making is that, for those willing to make the effort, our physical and spiritual bodies can be considered to be one and it is possible to develop the gifts of the spirit and act in ways unknown to the average person.

We need to be careful when trying to reach out beyond what we consider to be the limits of our dimension and into the unknown because our imagination can play tricks on us and present nonsense that we assume to be fact and also, our arch enemies, the Archons, are never far away and, if they can pick up the thoughts of a weak minded person, will distract any thoughts and create a history designed to lead us all down the garden path, to use a colloquialism.

We have spoken about illusion before but, perhaps, it will be worth mentioning this again so that we can better separate so-called fact from fiction but, although this is a very important topic in its own right, we do not wish to spend too long on it as we wish to examine the different world that we hope to bring to your attention.

But it is important to be able to tell if the information we are receiving is coming from our Higher Self (the source of all knowledge), or from imagination.

We will say that wisdom from the Higher Self has to pass through the imagination plane before arriving in our consciousness, so it is only too easy to stop using Higher Self and just let imagination feed us illusion.

If and when this happens we will be the last to know as imagination can present information in a very convincing manner.

What we are going to say here we have already told you but we feel obliged to repeat it as we try to explain this different universe which is the subject of this book. Those who try to contact that world must be able to differentiate between fact and fiction.

Fact comes from the Higher Self but fiction can come from a number of sources; imagination, "collective wisdom", and from the Archons and other entities who gain pleasure from misleading us.

The only source of wisdom is Higher Self. Anything else must be suspect.

The problem is, of course, how do we differentiate between information coming from Higher Self and that coming from another area?

There is only one way.

The master Jesus gave us the answer when he said "be still and know that I am".

This rather enigmatic statement has often been misconstrued.

By, "Be still", he meant to still the imagination plane.

By, "know that I am", he implied to allow information to pass from Higher Self, through imagination and into the mind unaltered by imagination.

He suggested that we should still imagination so that wisdom from Higher Self can reach us unaltered.

This can only be done through meditation. True meditation is the act of stopping our normal mind functions, which is always connected to imagination, so that we create a direct path between Higher Self and mind.

We have talked about imagination before and have stated that it is constantly active and is a valuable tool to help us cope with life. But, like a lot of things, imagination is a good servant but a bad master. The problem is that it is very difficult to still imagination so, with most of us, both discarnate and incarnate, imagination is constantly active and trying to push ideas at us, ideas that imagination has itself created.

Therefore, we can see that imagination has created virtually all that exists. But this strange force – imagination – can be so powerful that it appears real and solid.

Whatever dimension one lives in, imagination creates a form of solidity and, normally, it is only when one can rise above the level of that reality that it disappears only to be replaced by a new one as we do not like to live in true reality which is nothing.

We have, of course, mentioned over and over again that imagination creates our apparent reality but it is worth repeating so that we can start to understand that true reality is just an empty void.

The only reason that we create realities is so that we can gain experience. If we all lived in an empty void it would be quite impossible to have experiences except, possibly, of being permanently bored by that type of experience so we create the worlds we live in, in order to give our lives purpose.

This continues indefinitely into the future. Long after our Earthly incarnations are over we continue into reality after reality as we progress through the realms of light and wonder, all created by imagination of one sort or another: individual, collective or that created by Archangels for our experience.

Now, what has all this got to do with the subject of this book, which is to explain a different reality?

Quite simply, it is essential to have a firm foundation of understanding one reality in order to be able to relate to a new one. If someone was confused about one reality he would not be able to appreciate (delineate) where that reality left off and a new one started.

So, we have spent a great deal of time and effort to explain as many aspects of the realities we think exist in order to be able to compare all these realities to the new ones we wish to explain.

We hope that you can appreciate why we have labored the points of our realities, interesting as they are, in order to be able to wipe the slate clean and start again, so to speak.

Let us consider why there should be alternative realities of which you have never heard and are unknown to virtually all people.

We have explained about alternative realities including what are referred to as parallel realities, created as back up plans should any one reality fail and we have even mentioned the strange reality on the other side of nothingness (God).

But we have also suggested that creation is endless.

The reason for this is that creation is, indeed, endless and long before there was any form of reality that we can relate to there was more creation.

We need to stretch our minds back long before the so called "Big Bang" which created our universes – which we have explained in a previous book and told you that it is all a copy of a higher version of creation and is placed in the 6th dimension, that of imagination.

But before that there was another version of creation.

By saying this we do not mean to imply that before the "Big Bang" there was an empty void, we wish to imply that before the "Big Bang" our galaxies did not exist, the void did not exist because it had not yet been created but in another area of life an entirely different reality had been created and was just as full of life as this one is.

Now, we are going to explain this again in very simple terms to make sure that you can follow our thoughts.

So, please bear with us as we say again that what we call creation at one point did not exist. It all suddenly appeared and is called the "Big Bang"

In fact, it was a copy/paste from a different dimension as we have explained.

But it is assumed that before the "Big Bang" there was an empty void where our various galaxies are. This is not true.

Before the "Big Bang" nothing existed. There was no empty void.

You have to imagine that before everything that we now see was created, there was just nothing in what we call our reality.

This is a difficult concept to comprehend. Many people assume that before the "Big Bang" there was an empty space rather like having an empty room awaiting the moment when it is furnished.

This is not so. Before the "Big Bang" nothing at all existed. No space, no vacuum, no concept of an empty void. Nothing existed.

But, in a different concept, there was creation: there has always been creation. The trouble is that dimensions, or rather, subdimensions are endless and so it is, perhaps, not surprising that in these other subdimensions there is creation.

Of course, although these subdimensions have been proposed by some people, it is quite impossible for humans incarnate to imagine them and even less, to visit them.

However, we have different access to information and some very advanced beings have been able to visit some of them and have described what they have seen and experienced.

We should say that we are not referring to life as we have described it in other talks. We refer to life in a different way.

All that we have mentioned in all our books, essays, and talks have all been directly or indirectly connected to reality that we know, from the concept of the 8 carrier waves created by God to life in all the dimensions. That is all connected in one way or another. But we now wish you to forget all that while we attempt to explain a totally different concept of creation.

CHAPTER 2

LEAVING HOME

So, we leave all that we know, can imagine or think we might know and step into the unknown. Rather like leaving a house in which we have lived all our lives, with our families, friends, enemies and all that we have explored and step into the unknown.
We wish you fully to comprehend that before God created the 8 frequency bands, sometimes called dimensions, eons ago, there was life.
We cannot really call it "life elsewhere" because the concept of "elsewhere" implies that there was an elsewhere to go to. We also imply that elsewhere is outside of a known area.
This is not how it works.
The essential point to bear in mind, if we can, is that this force that we call God; the creative force, the all that is, is not an old man sitting on a cloud surveying us. God is an invisible, unmeasurable, unquantifiable force that nevertheless exists but exists in a void that contains absolutely nothing but God itself.
How many of us can really imagine that the most powerful force that has ever existed – will ever exist – living in an area where there is absolutely nothing?
Nothing at all. No space, no time, no gravity, nothing that even the most advanced physicist, mathematician or philosophers could describe.
God is a force that does not exist in any way imaginable to even the most advanced of us and yet lives, and lives in an area like himself which does not exist in any understandable way.
So, this strange creative force created everything in his image which is to say that everything; you, me, us, all life in any area or dimension exists just as a force.
You, extraordinary as this seems, exist only as an imaginary concept. The real you is God, and thus, the real you is something that could never be seen, measured, quantified or understood and yet you also exist as the totality of all life. You, as an individual, contain the essence of all life, everywhere, from the moment of your creation by God to the moment you return to God. And yet, if we could strip away the layers of imaginary existence, rather like peeling an onion, at your core you exist as an unmeasurable force living in an unmeasurable "somewhere" that we can say does not exist. So, you are a "something" – a nothing – existing in a somewhere – nowhere – and yet you are also the totality of everything – of all creation. If you did not exist, nothing would exist because you are all that exists. And this existence does not exist, not even as a concept, because you are God, the totality of God, the all that is, and yet you both exist and do not exist at the same time. It is obvious that you exist or you would not be reading this book but the force that animates you does not seem to exist in any quantifiable or imaginable manner.

This apparent gobbledygook is actually a great truth. It is the fundamental truth – the only original truth – and yet it is so strange, even to advanced beings elsewhere in the cosmos, that no one really understands.

Who, in all honesty could say that they understand that all that exists in every corner of the cosmos cannot actually exist because the force that creates it all does not seem to exist?

And yet even this cannot be true because, if what we see around us, and in all dimensions everywhere in this unbelievably huge multidimensional existence does indeed exist, even in our imagination, there has to be some force that creates it even in imaginary form.

So, we clearly have a gap in our knowledge that no one anywhere, ever, has filled.

So, we have various names for this force; God, the all that is, our Father and so on and we just accept. That is all we can say.

So where does this take us?

The simple truth is that this force we refer to as God has always existed and has always been active, creating universe after universe.

Now, let us try to expand on this concept and see if we can bring any clarity to it.

We said that God has always existed. That is a bold statement to make as we can have absolutely no concept of what existed before the 8 carrier wave bands that God created long ago that has resulted in the worlds we see around us.

This is not quite true.

It has been possible to contact certain human Archangels as opposed to those who work for creation – and these human Archangels have informed us that they have information beyond the level of our information.

They have told us that God has always existed and that God has created reality after reality stretching back unimaginable lengths of time.

The reason that these Archangels have this information is quite simply, being so pure, they have a direct link to God and thus have access to all the information that God has stored in his memory, information about the other universes he has created. But, being human, they retain a link with us and share knowledge with us.

So, much of what we are going to tell you in this book has come from these human Archangels to whom we all share a debt of gratitude.

The big and unanswerable question, of course, is that why has God always existed? Was there any other force in existence before God that created God?

We, like you, question these things and we, like you, can find no answer.

Just how long a period of time "always" refers to is also a mystery. Of course, as time does not exist, at least in our universe and there is only the "now" moment, we could say that God only exists in this "now" moment and that would be true but, somehow, common sense tells us that is just a way of avoiding the question.

Who is to say that in other universes created by God before our one, time did not exist?

Who is to say that if sequence of events exists, which is another way of looking at time, life did not go back and back like in time.

There is no point in guessing. We are informed by beings we trust (human Archangels) that God has always existed so we must just accept this as true although we will admit that it leaves us with a bad taste in our mouths – if you will forgive the expression – to have to accept something that defies logic and cannot be answered.

12

We like to think that all things have a logical beginning and a logical progression so to say that God has always existed is a struggle to accept.

But there are things like that, a classic one being, "which came first the chicken or the egg"?

We wish we had the answer to that puzzle but we don't.

We have to accept that a chicken lays fertilized eggs, covre's them and, eventually, beautiful chicks appear.

How that sequence of events was brought into being we don't know.

Fortunately, there are few things that are inexplicable and with time, perhaps we will find the answers but for the moment we must just accept that we do not have all the answers.

But, we do understand something about other realities outside of our one and we will return to trying to explain one of them.

So, we must go back to a time before our universe, our dimensions, our version of reality in all its shapes and forms existed. We return to the moment that we have already attempted to describe when absolutely nothing existed, no space, no time, absolutely nothing.

But now let us with our imaginations try to feel that we exist and are able to transcend this nothingness until we voyage through nothingness to a something. A something that existed in another concept of life.

Let us, with our minds attempt to approach this distant reality rather as if we were leaving our galaxy in a craft of some sort, traversing empty space to approach a different galaxy. This analogy is quite apt, the main difference being that instead of crossing empty space between our galaxy and a far different one, we are crossing some barrier between two realities.

Now, we feel obliged to try to describe, if we can, what we mean by two different realities.

Obviously, words and concepts do not exist accurately to describe leaving one reality and entering another so we can only use analogies in feeble attempts to describe what we mean.

We don't know if you have ever left a busy, bustling, modern city and traveled to a very "primitive" area like a jungle, a desert community or similar. The contrast can be quite astonishing as we leave so call civilization and find ourselves in an area where survival is all that matters.

This is not to imply that the people who live in these undeveloped areas are in anyway less intelligent than city dwellers. These people develop different skill sets and live by different rules.

So, as we leave our reality and approach a different reality, we would expect life to live by different skill sets and different aims and objectives to the reality that we just left behind.

We hope that you have clearly understood what we are saying. The galaxy, the multiverse in which all of us have lived in since it was all first created by God long, long ago, is just one of an endless creation of realities stretching back endlessly and, no doubt, stretching forward endlessly and we are attempting to describe – or will be – one totally detached from our reality and yet, we hope, sufficiently close in many ways that we can use language to explain what we see.

We understand that there are other multiverses so different from ours that words do not exist to describe them.

CHAPTER 3

A STICKY PROBLEM

After that rather long and drawn out introduction in which we attempted to introduce the concept of realities created by God but in no way connected to our reality, let us approach, in our minds, one of them and devote the rest of this book to a description of the closest reality to ours. We deliberately chose this reality because, as we said, words do not exist to describe other realities.

So, let us imagine that we are in a craft that was able to cross nothingness (the gap between our reality and the new one) rather as if aliens did much the same from their galaxy to ours and their dimension to ours.

Just as aliens from a different dimension, when they enter our dimension have the choice of a vast number of planets, moons, etc, they could visit, so as we approach this new reality we are faced with choices.

But, the choices in our chosen destination are not quite like the choices that aliens would have as they visit our galaxy. It seems that in this different reality planets as we know them do not exist. Space – the vacuum between planets in our reality – does not exist, there would be no point in space existing.

But we now enter an area somewhat difficult to describe.

As we approach this new reality, from afar (if we could step back enough) we would see it as a monstrous ball of glowing light just hanging in nothingness.

This is not easy to imagine but try if you will.

So, picture an empty space with no life, no gravity, no light, no dark, no time, no past, present or future. That is the "nothing" that we encountered when we left our reality with all its suns, stars, planets, space, dimensions and so on.

We can't say that we traveled across this nothingness because there was nothing to cross. But it seems that some human Archangels have been able to make this adjustment, this leap in the dark, and have seen this ball of light.

We have to try also to imagine that this ball of light is not a small object. It is galaxy sized but exists as a monstrous ball of light.

It must be said that if we could step far enough out into space to be able to observe our galaxy, it also would be seen as a spherical object. It appears that a heavy object, providing it is malleable enough, naturally takes the form of a sphere which is why, molten lead dropped from a tower into a tub of cold water forms balls that were used in guns years ago.

It also could, if people's minds were open enough, put a stop once and for all to this "flat Earth" concept that is going the rounds in some areas.

As a sphere is the shape of the galaxy in this different reality and also our galaxy and, indeed, virtually all the planets, moons, and suns within it are spherical, that is a primary shape, which at least gives us a starting point to which we can relate.

However, we are not implying that this different galaxy - or multiverse as we might term it – contains solid bodies like stars, planets, moons, etc., as seen in our multiverse.

We are talking about a different reality.

So, we observe, from afar, this ball of light.

We should, perhaps, break off here to explain why it is seen as a ball of light although anyone who has followed our various writings up until now should be able to work out the answer for themselves.

But for those who cannot let us provide the answer.

Everything is made by and from God.

Now, we have stated that God does not exist in any fashion that could be described so we must content ourselves with a description of the effects, as seen, of the power of God and that effect is light – star light.

This is a basic truth although we will say that the brightness of this light and its color can be modified by consciousness of those manipulating that light.

Heaven glows with light while hell gets dimmer and dimmer as the beings that live in hell modify that light with their dark and dismal thoughts.

In its present form, the pure light of God is seen as star light. If we were to go outside of Earth's atmosphere into space, the brightness of that light is extraordinary. But we humans are looking at starlight through the filters of a human's ability to observe with eyes and also it is modified by our level of spirituality. If we were able to see star light with pure astral vision, the brightness and purity of whiteness would be breathtaking. However, when we look at the brightness and purity of the light of this new galaxy it is noticed that it is not as bright as pure star light which immediately suggests to us that; (a) there must be life forms in that galaxy and (b) those life forms might not be of total purity.

As we said, consciousness modifies spiritual light so we note, with interest, that the life forms contained within this ball of light might be somewhat like those we know to be in our reality, which is to say some good, some evil and some in between. Thus, we make the assumption that life here might well be like in our reality which is to say a sort of school for the development of young souls. But we are only guessing as we have not yet started to explore life here so we might well be jumping to hasty and wrong conclusions. We hope that by the time we get to the end of this book, which is to say, at the end of our exploration of this new reality we will have a clearer picture.

So, we approach this ball of light and see what a closer look might reveal. We approach with caution. It would be most unwise to just plunge into the ball of light without first trying to ascertain something about it.

We circumnavigate the exterior and take measurements of the temperature, of atmosphere, try to ascertain any gases that we are familiar with and we do note some similarities.

We become aware that, although the temperature varies somewhat, it would be quite amenable to life as we know it in our world – planet Earth. This raises certain questions because if we were to try to conduct similar measurements from the outside of our galaxy, we would notice vast differences. Although on planet Earth we find temperatures and gases generally conductive to life as we know it, the same cannot be said for the rest of the galaxy with its vast areas of near total vacuum, planets, some icy cold, some ferociously hot and many areas that we would have difficulty in trying to understand using conventional measuring devices and with the limited knowledge that we have.

But this galaxy sized ball of light appears different.
From what we can measure from the exterior it seems to be a cohesive whole with very little variation.
This is strange and defies logic.
From our point of view, we would easily accept a small ball that has one temperature, made up, or at least containing, a limited number of gases rather like a melon or a similar object but we cannot readily accept a galaxy sized object with such a limited diversity of features.
We wonder if this ball of light is unfinished, a work in progress (to use a modern term) and the beings creating it have not yet completed their work.
But, at the same time, if this ball was created long before our reality had been made, and our reality seems fairly well thought out, one would have thought that this reality had also been finished, so we ponder the possibility that this is what the creators had in mind when they created it.
So, this begs the question as to who created it and for what purpose?

We accept that the mind of God is behind all creation and God creates this for his own development so we assume that he created Archangels of various types to implement his thoughts and bring them into some sort of reality.
After all, that was and is the way that our reality came into being.
But we also know that the mind of God is infinite and his quest for knowledge is endless so we must be careful not to make comparisons, to assume that just because Archangels made our galaxy with all its diverse dimensions that the same is true for a new (or old) galaxy in a different reality.
Perhaps God did not use Archangels to create this place. Perhaps God used a totally different technique to bring it into being.
This gives us a fascinating opportunity to expand our knowledge and to grow in stature if we can intelligently investigate this new world and uncover its secrets.

Where to begin?
We can only use our intelligence and fall back on the techniques that ancient explorers used when arriving, after a long sea crossing, at a previously unknown land mass.
They would anchor their ships out to sea in safe waters and row ashore onto a beach.
From there they might well set up a sort of base camp and then start to explore the land that lead away from the beach.
But can we do the same with this strange galaxy?
We approach the edge of the ball of light and, no matter how carefully we scan into the ball of light, we can discover no planets as we know them, no land masses. Not even any seas or anything to which we could relate and, certainly, nowhere where we could land and explore even a small part of it on foot.

All we are able to see is light. And yet, closer observation shows us that this light is not quite static like a huge light bulb. It is scintillating, sparkling, some parts of it shining more brightly than others.

How to explain?

Imagine that you were looking at a lit ball of light that had, floating inside it, a large number of tiny dust particles swirling endlessly about. Try to imagine the effect that you would observe – a sphere of light but the dust particles creating the effect that the whole sphere was shimmering.

This is what this galaxy looks like from the outside at first glance.

So, to make sure you have the image clearly visible in your minds we will repeat.

We have discovered suspended in a "nowhere place" where nothing at all exists, a galaxy sized ball of light just suspended in nothingness.

Further, this ball of light is shimmering as if a huge amount of particles of dust were gently, slowly swirling around in this ball at random.

Closer inspection reveals that it is not the sphere that is glowing but what appears to be the particles of dust that are emitting light of various degrees of various hues, some quite bright, some very dim. Some white and others of different colors.

We also appreciate that we are looking from afar at a galaxy sized ball and so what appears to be dust particles are actually planet sized spheres of light swirling around in this huge ball.

This is a somewhat comforting realization because we are used, in our galaxy, to seeing planets so this gives us – we hope – a point of reference.

So, we pluck up our courage and plunge into this galaxy sized sphere.

As we do so we have the impression that the space between any two particles of dust, which we now realize are planets, of sorts, is actually a fairly thick jelly like structure.

We have some difficulty in progressing through this jelly – which is actually invisible to us – and, if we stop, we remain suspended within it and start to drift about, seemingly at random, much as the planets do.

We decide that, before progressing, we should try to define just what this jelly like substance is. So, we take our time and apply ourselves to examining this jelly.

After much consideration we come to the conclusion that it is a curious form of gravity.

Not like any gravity with which we are familiar but gravity nevertheless.

We question why this gravity should be so thick?

We puzzle this for some time before we come to any conclusion.

The problem is that we realize that we are in a creation (made by God) outside of any creation with which we are familiar and thus, God in his infinite desire to create life, must have had good reason to create this.

We also are aware that God has absolutely no desire to hide anything from us and, therefore, we should be able to puzzle this out.

After some discussion we come to the conclusion that we have never fully understood gravity.

If we think back to our 3D reality as applied to the creation in which we live, it crosses our mind that gravity is not a fixed power.

For instance, if we wish to cross the place (space) between any two points we can do it quite easily. We just walk across the space on Earth, for instance and, although we have the gravitation of pull of the Earth acting on us, it does not seem to prevent us from moving at all.

The same applies in the air. A bird can fly and, although it has gravity that is trying to pull the bird to Earth, the only resistance the bird really feels is that of air.
So, we think about air and realize that the elements of air, which are gases of various types, do not seem to be overly affected by gravity and thus remain suspended rather than all being drawn down to the surface of planet Earth which logic would suggest.

But we realize that stones and rocks remain fixed – to a certain degree – on Earth by gravity and even water, which is basically just a mixture of two gases, remains fixed to Earth.

So, we realize that, perhaps, gravity is more complex than at first sight.
We realize that it would be pointless continuing until we understand more about gravity as it applies to our galaxy before attempting to understand this version of gravity in this different reality.

Thus, we return to our 3D reality to try to unravel the secrets of gravity and then, perhaps we can return to the alternative world and understand the type of gravity that we found there.

So, we gather around us some wise souls and explain the jelly like gravity that we have found there. Much to our surprise we are told to examine an atom. So, we do.
What we discover is a sort of sphere with a varying number of points – of particles – floating in a sort of jelly like substance. We realize that, in all probability the galaxy we came across was a gigantic version of the very atoms that we encounter in our reality. Could it be that God had created an atom but of enormous proportions long ago and that when, with the aid of his Archangels, he created our galaxy, he used a miniature version of this atom to create the life that we experience?
But, of course, this does not explain why gravity is so thick in an atom but appears to be so thin on a macro scale.

We need to stretch our minds outside of what we think we know about gravity and realize that it is a spiritual force, created by the Archangels and designed to hold all life in balance. We are going to have to re-examine vibration, that we have mentioned so often, and try to examine what vibration, frequency (call it what you will) really is because this seems to be at the heart of everything.

We have mentioned that everything is vibration but we have also stated that everything is composed of atoms vibrating in certain ways to create all that exists.
We have said that not only are material things made of vibration but thoughts, ideas, concepts, hopes, ambitions, love, joy, fear and hate are all vibrations of different sorts.

We have also said that the atoms are also connected to these vibrations so all the above mentioned aspects contain atoms and all is alive. Life is all there is and life is both vibration but needs atoms to give that life a form of solidity. Thoughts are things – physical things, if we may use such an expression in abstract reality – so even thoughts and emotions require atoms to give those thoughts solidity.

It is probably difficult for many of you to appreciate that, as you think, so a stream of atoms are shooting out from you in astral form, passing through the 6th dimension and clothing your file in the Akashic Record rather as if we were spraying paint endlessly onto the walls of a room reserved exclusively for you.
Of course, this is just one of the many analogies we use but if it helps you to visualize that atoms are what go to make up the Akashic Record, we have helped you to understand.

So, can we link vibrations and atoms together and also link them to gravity?
We wish to point out that when we use the word atoms we are not just referring to those that you know of in physical form. Atoms are a fundamental part of the building blocks of all creation so there are far more atoms than science knows about. They exist in all dimensions and each atom, when it is in its quiescent form, not being used, vibrates to the quiescent frequency of whatever dimension it is attached to.
Further, not only is each atom to be found in a particular dimension, but all atoms have in association with them auras, which are aspects of the other dimensions.
Thus, we can say that each atom might well find itself in a particular dimension – its home base – but has, also, connections to all the other dimensions as does everything else.
Thus, we can say that all is one. If that is true, it implies that there cannot actually be separate atoms, separate objects all floating in a sea of gravity. We must assume that all is one point of life. Even this point of life cannot exist in any physical form nor even in any non-physical form. It just exists.

So, how can we possibly imagine this in any understandable fashion?
We think – we hope – that if you can imagine a vast something that appears to be a galaxy is, in fact, one item that has neither shape nor form in any physical or non-physical manner, then the atoms (or rather the "non-atoms") that constitute that non-object would all be held together by some force to create this non-object.
This, clearly, is beyond the imagination of most of us although we have mentioned this concept before in a previous work.
We must do so again because the force that holds all these non-objects together is the force we term gravity. So, unfortunately, we must say that if atoms do not actually exist and if the bodies that atoms combine to create do not exist then the force we call gravity cannot actually exist. If we visualize atoms, objects and the gravitational pull that holds them all together, we must just be using imagination.
Of course, we have stated that imagination is a real force and, therefore, must use atoms to create imagination but we have also stated that neither atoms nor gravity actually exists. Therefore, even imagination cannot exist.

20

The problem, as you can see, is that we are torn between two forms of apparent lunacy. On one hand we have the strange world that we have spent much time trying to explain, that we said was a sort of reality, even if imaginary, and on the other we are saying that nothing at all exists, even imaginary.

Those of you who have followed our teachings thus far over the years and have come to trust what we tell you as true, no matter how bizarre what we tell you might be, will surely falter at this point. How can everything not exist at all even in imagination, especially as we have spent years describing life? And now we are implying that life does not exist in any measurable, understandable form at all!

What we have stated is also true but is so advanced in physics that almost no one incarnate or even discarnate could possibly comprehend.
So, we will return to the previous step and imagine that life as we know it does exist.

CHAPTER 4

STRONG AND WEAK FORCE FIELDS

Thus, we return to the world that we know with its atoms combining due to gravity to form all that we see, all that seems to exist.

But we have got no further in solving the mystery of why gravity as we "observe" it seems to be a thin force, barely noticeable once atoms have combined to form an object and yet if we look into a single atom gravity seems to be much stronger and, although still invisible, appears to be much thicker. Of course, we understand that this force is invisible no matter how it manifests itself, and this thinness or thickness is just a way of describing the force, either weak or strong.

People that study atoms have noticed this and have described the force as weak or strong depending on the service it performs.

So, something is not only creating gravity but is able to manipulate it to provide a force that can vary in intensity according to the use required.

We assume it must be the incredible Archangels who work directly for God that create this and must have a very good reason for ranging this force or, we further assume, knowing them to be of incredible intelligence they would not waste energy in so doing.

Therefore, if this force with all its variations has been created it should be possible to find out the "secret" as everything created is using physics in one form or another.

There is no magic involved, it is just a case of understanding the physics involved.

So, we notice that the larger the object seems to be the weaker the gravitational force used upon it.

By which we mean that a planet the size of the Earth, Mars, Jupiter, Saturn for example can be held in Orbit around the sun by an extremely weak gravitational quantity but the interior of a miniscule atom contains a great deal of gravity.

This would seem to be the opposite of what logic would indicate.

Any common sense would suggest that to keep huge planets whirling around in space nevertheless in a certain proximity to the sun would require an enormous quantity of gravity where as a tiny atom would require very little gravity to keep it all in place.

Indeed, logic would suggest that the further the planet was from the sun, the greater the gravitational force that would be required to keep it in orbit and to stop it flying off out into the cosmos.

Clearly there is an aspect of gravity, of life that we haven't understood.

So, our task is to try to comprehend this strange force.

Once again, we turn to our colleagues much more evolved than us and they provide us with answers, as far as they, themselves, understand.

We are told that gravity is part of the fundamental building system of creation, part of the system that was created long ago when the 8 dimensions were made.

We know that these dimensions are vibrations, of variations of star light, the force of God itself.

If we take just one dimension, we understand that a dimension is not just one frequency. It is a band of frequencies. Although it is actually quite impossible to know the frequencies involved, let us use a knowledge of frequencies as used on Earth and say that any dimension is composed of a band of related frequencies rising from, say, one Hertz to one hundred Hertz. We want you to clearly understand that what we say is merely to explain in simple terms and has no basis in any reality.

So, let us imagine that what we call a dimension is created of a vibration of one Hertz (one cycle per second) crossing the void that is part of creation.

Next to it is another vibration of two Hertz and next to that is another of three Hertz and so on up to one hundred. These hundred different vibrations constitute what we call a dimension.

Something must be constructed – invented – to hold these hundred, disparate frequencies together as one band to constitute a dimension or they would just be different frequencies floating about with no connection, one to another.

But they must be held together to make a composite whole that we refer to as a dimension.

In a way they must be "glued" together.

This glue is what we call gravity and was invented by the Archangels to keep the frequencies together as a composite construction.

So, we have a number of frequencies, each one different from another and each one held close to each other by some glue that we call gravity and each one constitutes, collectively, what is referred to as a dimension.

Now, there are two versions of this glue (gravity). There is a version that holds each frequency connected to the others and then there is a second type of gravity that envelopes all of the frequencies, combined, and encases them in a sort of protective sheath.

We will explain this again as, to understand gravity, it is necessary to understand this aspect of it.

We will explain in a slightly different way.

Imagine, if you will, a group of wires put together for some purpose; to pass electricity of different powers, to pass independent telephone conversations or whatever.

Imagine a long series of wires, each one serving a common but unique purpose placed one next to the other. Imagine each wired glued to the next, or encased in some material to hold them together as is found in "Ribbon Cable" or something similar. The glue or material holding them, insulated one from another, but connected together we refer to as one type of gravity.

But then imagine a protective coating placed outside of the group of wires to keep all the wires grouped as one band of wires, of frequencies.

So, what we call a dimension is a large series of frequencies, of vibrations, each one independent from the others but held together as one band and then, covering the whole lot of frequencies, a coating that groups all of these frequencies together so that they will never become confused with any other frequencies.

The independent frequencies are grouped by one type of gravity and the external coating is a second type of gravity.

The questions are, of course, why should there be two types of gravity and what roles do they play in life?

As always, there is the simple answer and the more complicated one.

The weak form of gravity is the one that holds the individual strands – vibrations – linked, one next to the other and the strong one is the gravity that holds all the different frequencies bundled together to create a dimension.

We think that, if we go on with our analogy of a number of wires glued one next to another, we can see that we would not need a very powerful glue to hold them in place but that it would be a great advantage to have all these strands protected together so that no one strand could ever become detached from the whole group. A strong gravity.

Thus, we have these two types of gravity.

But what has that to do with "real" life, with planets orbiting the sun and the interior of a miniscule atom?

Everything is made of vibration but everything has a unique vibration.

Now, the sun is vibrating at a particular frequency and each and every planet vibrates to a particular, unique vibration.

To take the case of planet Earth, for instance, it vibrates to a unique vibration different from any other planet anywhere in creation. Everything is doing the same (vibrating to its own vibration or frequency).

But the planet is made of atoms. It is important that each atom is kept together in a bond almost unbreakable. To create an atom which, when there is enough of them, creates an object, each atom needs to maintain at all costs its integrity. Should the molecules that link together to form an atom lose that integrity and the atom fall apart, or split, as it is called, the result could be catastrophic. We see the result in nuclear explosions where a vast amount of highly dangerous radioactivity is released or again, in a certain collider, where atoms are forced apart in a very crude fashion on the pretext of observing the dawns of time.

As all atoms contain auras which, themselves are glued to the molecule and to the atom itself by gravity, to rip them apart not only creates damage on Earth but does so in other dimensions as a knock-on effect occurs throughout the auras connected to an atom.

Auras being just another word for dimensions, so when atoms are damaged, dimensions are also.

In order for an atom to maintain its integrity, the strong glue or gravity is used. However, atoms vibrate to the quiescent frequency of that atom and also to the frequency of the object they create.

We break off here to say that it seems unlikely that anything could vibrate to two separate but related frequencies at the same time but we will explain at some point in this book. Atoms and how they combine to create objects are far more complicated than science has yet discovered so we will need to explain carefully and now is not the moment to begin that discussion.

So, we have an atom that requires to vibrate freely but, at the same time, needs to be always linked to all the other atoms that combine to constitute and object.
Thus, the weak gravitational force is used that permits a certain degree of elasticity enabling each atom to vibrate at the requested frequency.
But the interior of each atom is held in a firm grip to maintain its integrity. Thus, strong gravity is used inside each atom and weak gravity is used to link each atom to the next one, enabling each atom to vibrate or swing about but remain within the formed object.

Therefore, if we imagine a ball, for instance, a solid ball. There are countless atoms, held as an atom by a strong gravity, but each atom free to vibrate but locked to all the other atoms by a weak gravitational force.

However, the exterior of the ball is coated, if we may thus describe it, by a strong gravitational field that maintains the ball as a solid spherical object.

To explain again, a solid ball is made of atoms. Within each atom are a number of molecules. These molecules are kept within the atom by a strong gravitational force. Thus, we might visualize each atom as a tiny ball. This is not actually true and just used as an example.
Then each atom is able to have a certain space around it so that it can vibrate (swing about).
We have countless atoms, each one swinging in all directions but held together and apart by a weak gravitational force.
Finally, in order for the ball to retain its integrity as a ball, a strong gravitational field envelopes the ball and thus it retains its shape and we observe a ball

We do not see the ball vibrating, pulsing to the frequency of the dimension in which it is placed because we too are in that dimension, thus are vibrating at the same frequency as the ball.
Nor can we observe or measure the individual atoms, each one vibrating or swinging in its own tiny space. We just see a ball. It appears solid to our eyes and to the touch but science knows that all objects are mainly empty space. This is the space required for each atom to swing freely with sufficient space so that no two atoms touch. If they did, unfortunate effects would occur as has been noted in the Hadron Collider where they so unwisely are deliberately causing atoms to smash into each other.
This act is a violation of nature and should never be performed.
If it were not for the fact that the scientists have had the wisdom (if one can call it that) to contain the effects within a limited space by enormous electromagnets, which are a form of gravity, the knock on effect in all dimensions would be catastrophic.

We do not criticize the motives of these scientists nor do we question their true motives, but we are grateful that there are advanced beings from a number of dimensions that have been attracted to that area and monitor the experiments ready to step in if things should get out of hand and take steps to limit the damage.

Free will requires that science must experiment but science will not be allowed to cause incredible harm to the world and to all the dimensions.

It is most unwise to tamper with nature unless one has sufficient knowledge to understand the physics involved and the limits to which one should push experiments.

Life is both complicated and for a strange reason, the more one seems to examine the micro aspects of it, the more each atom or element seems to contain immense power.

It is as if the secrets contained in the most fundamental aspects of life were designed to remain locked away from prying eyes – unless and until the moment would arrive when man was ready to understand these building blocks.

We strongly feel that God's Archangels would never wish for anything to remain secret permanently, but we do realise that man has to grow both intellectually and spiritually before he is ready to stand shoulder to shoulder with the creative powers and wonders in the glory of creation revealed to him.

But we were examining gravity and came to the conclusion that there were two types of gravity, strong and weak.

We could, we suppose, question why gravity exists at all but even the most curious of us must realise that gravity works in conjunction with the first - or one of the first - laws of the universe, like attracts like, the law of mutual attraction.

We realize that if it were not for this simple rule, things being drawn together that, over time, has formed all that is, nothing as we know it would exist.

We further can easily see that the Archangels, who constructed everything according to God's prime desire, created gravity as a means of drawing matter together.

So, gravity is a spiritual law that has been transformed in a sort of physical force that works to keep all material things in their place. We further realize through the crude experiments conducted by unwise people that somewhere in this combination – matter and gravity – is contained an immense force that can be so destructive if released in haphazard fashion.

We realize that the aim of this book was to examine the strange reality that we had discovered and that we started to describe earlier.

But we feel that it is, perhaps, time to try to get to grips with just what gravity is and we hope that you will excuse us if we take a few pages to try to explain what we know about gravity as it is very important to the immediate future here on Earth as man starts to learn how to manipulate gravity in his attempts to create flying craft known as flying saucers, using antigravity techniques, and also we hope an understanding of gravity will help us explore the aforementioned galaxy in a different reality that we had discovered.

We hope that our understanding of gravity will help us forge a link between that world and ours.

So, gravity, as we mentioned is a spiritual force connected to our reality.

Let us explain just what we mean by spiritual. This is where words do not exist to explain a force that is both created by God's Archangels, but at the same time will be, one day, measurable using physics.

We could say that gravity is a non-physical force, which is a term that we have used before when trying to describe something that existed in non-corporeal sense.

Yet even this is not true.

Gravity might well exist as a non-physical force but it's effects are very physical indeed, operating ceaselessly on every atom, every molecule contains within every atom without end.

So, we will try to note on paper what we know about gravity so far – and it is not much.

1. Gravity was invented – created – by God's Archangels so as to draw matter together according to the law of mutual attraction. Thus, it is what we call a spiritual concept.

2. Gravity has a form of physical reality in that it's effects on matter is real, keeping all things in their place. It will one day be measured when man has invented tools able to reach out into areas beyond known physics.

3. There are two forms of gravity, strong and weak, although we have not yet discovered how any object knows which form of gravity it requires.

That, in a nutshell is about all we know concerning gravity up till this point. Anything else anyone could add to those three statements would just be variations of those three things.

However, let us not be dismayed by this apparent mystery concerning gravity.

We understand that if man so far has not yet uncovered much about gravity and yet we see visitors from other areas whizzing through both the sky and through dimensions with apparent nonchalance, they must have understood gravity sufficiently to master it and to nullify its effects.

Actually, all this concerning alien visitors gives us some clues concerning gravity.

If it is true that what we call aliens come from places that we have not yet visited, they are probably coming from areas that we call dimensions, either from another part of our dimensions or from dimensions we might refer to as alternative realities.

We just break off at this point for a moment to state, not for the first time, that there is no life as we might describe it on the surface of any planet, at least in our galaxy.

All the stories of alien life coming from galaxies light years away, are stories made up either by Earth scientists wishing to pull the wool over your eyes, or by the aliens themselves wishing to do the same or by people's imagination. All non-terrestrial life comes from dimensions which are many, varied and virtually unknown to the general public.

One can see why aliens and the secret governments who interact with these aliens find it easy to let people think that life exists on other planets than have to start quite complicated physics lessons to the public in an attempt to explain dimensions.

Also, it must be said that it has been easier to deny alien visitation by stating that even at the speed of light it would take impossibly long periods of time for aliens to get here.

This reassures the public who would naturally be frightened of unknown beings suddenly appearing amongst us.

For some reason, the idea of beings from dimensions invisible to us seems frightening. The Bible and other religious texts has gone to great lengths to put into people's minds that there are only two forces – God and the Devil. If anything lives in an invisible area, it must be the devil or his acolytes.

However, we hope that you who have followed our teachings thus far can appreciate that life is not always so simple: Black and/or white, good or evil.

Most things are shades of grey.

Let us return to the subject of gravity and see if we can uncover some of the grey areas that remain to be discovered.

One area we might look at is the area or subject of two types of gravity.

With most things, they are seldom one or the other. There are usually shades in between. People are not either strong or weak. There are degrees of strength. Materials are not strong or weak. There are always materials in stages between strong and weak.

So, it is possible that there are degrees of strength concerning gravity and, if so, can we find out these degrees and describe them?

Well, we can cut a long story short and tell you that there are. People in the heavenly spheres have studied gravity for a long time and, although they have not yet managed to discover all the answers, have answered some of the questions.

We apologise for the somewhat childish manner in which we have described gravity but it is a subject not at all easy to describe and we felt that we should describe gravity in as easy to understand manner as possible so that all could comprehend.

We were discussing gravity and trying to find out if there were shades of strength. We stated that there were.

Actually, gravity was mentioned in the first book we gave you (Stairway to Freedom) and we did explain somewhat but, for those who have not read that book we will describe again.

What we are going to state, you will have to take on trust, because we can present no proof to you of what we are going to describe. Science has not yet invented the tools to measure what we are going to tell you.

And it is this.

Atoms are not the fixed quantities we imagine. Or rather it is the gravitational force surrounding atoms that is not fixed.

We have mentioned in another book that atoms are created each one for a specific use. We told you that, of all the atoms surrounding a person, only those atoms that would contribute to that person's growth, health or ability to survive would be attached to him. That is because those atoms would be endowed with the same vibrational frequency as that person.

All other atoms would have other vibrations corresponding to the frequency of other things, animal, vegetable, or mineral and would only be attracted to that person, animal or object. All other atoms would remain floating in space until called in to assist some person, animal or object.

So, can you see that all the countless atoms in creation, each and every atom is stamped with a unique frequency corresponding, uniquely, to something or someone. Each atom, regardless of whether it be made into Oxygen, Hydrogen, or whatever, has a unique destiny. Thus, of all the atoms of, say Oxygen, floating in space, only those corresponding to your frequency will be drawn to you.

This is an amazing fact that we described in an earlier book and has, no doubt, been largely ignored by people who have other things on their minds rather than to worry about atoms.

But we wish to state something else that we have already mentioned in this first book. Not only has each atom a stamp that tells it that it is reserved for you, just to use "you" as an example, but each atom, or should we say the gravitational force, is adjusted to conform to your requirements.

The same is for all things. Thus, the atoms that constitute a stone, for example, have a greater gravitational force than similar atoms that go into making a feather or a bone of a bird.

A stone needs to be heavy to provide the weight (mass) of a planet and thus requires the atoms to be heavier than the same atoms that make up a bird.

Conversely, the atoms which constitute a bird have much less gravity than those of a stone so that the bird can fly.

We wish to convey to you that, with regard to atoms or the various elements that combine to create an atom it is not the quantity of elements contained in an atom that contribute to its weight (mass), it is the gravitational field surrounding the atoms that give it its apparent mass.

Each atom has a gravitational field that is carefully calculated and adjusted to correspond to the use to which each atom is put.

So, as we said, a stone appears to be heavier than a bird's feather.

A question has sprung up regarding the concept that, in a vacuum, a hammer would fall to Earth at the same velocity as a feather. It was demonstrated when man went to the moon. We will only say that this was a conjurer's trick set up to give the impression that the astronauts were on the moon at that time.

Gravity is quite independent of space. Therefore, it is true that the gravitational attraction between a feather and planet Earth can be affected by the aerodynamic form of the feather – an effect that would be nullified in a vacuum – but it would be the force that a hammer would hit the ground compared to a feather that denotes the gravitational attraction between planet Earth and any objects falling towards it.

The magnetic pull between a hammer and the Earth, the result of a large amount of gravity contained within or rather around each atom of the hammer would cause it to strike the Earth with a considerable force compared to a feather that would scarcely make a mark.

This gravitational force relevant to all things is calculated by our now familiar friends, the Archangels that work for the God force, ably aided by the Directors of Life.

There is a further aspect of gravity that we must consider, and that is the elastic band effect.

It has been noted that if a hammer were dropped from a very short distance from the surface of the Earth – or from someone's feet – it does not drop with much force but, if the same hammer was dropped from a considerable height it would strike Earth – or someone's foot – with a great force, resulting in a dent in the Earth or several squashed toes!

We must question why this should be?

The answer is that gravity is not a constant effect.

It acts as if it were alive and sentient, which, of course, it is. All things are alive including a hammer and gravity.

Life can take many forms.

The atoms that constitute a hammer were originally from Earth – iron ore. So that gravitational field that surrounds each atom of the iron ore, and its various other Earthly minerals, would have been given great strength so that the iron ore can constitute part of the mass of Earth, the foundation of life to incarnate to. So, iron ore always retains its apparent heaviness.

Here is the amazing part.

If we take a piece of iron ore up into the sky, although the piece of iron ore itself does not alter in weight, the attractive force between the Earth and a piece of it that has been detached (the iron ore) increases.

The easiest way to imagine this is to visualize an elastic band that, as you stretch it, the resistance grows more and more. That, of course, is the concept behind a catapult that projects a stone a considerable distance before the stone falls to Earth.

So, a hammer taken into the sky falls, not at a linear speed but at an ever increasing speed as the increased gravitational pull between Earth and the hammer tugs it back to its home, Earth.

There is a limit to the elastic band effect as the apparent gravity only stretches so far. We should explain this.

Archangels never waste energy, so when they calculate the amount of attractive force, called gravity, that is required for any atom that will, at some stage, constitute a "something" whatever that something might be, they endow each and every atom with sufficient gravity for it to accomplish its task successfully.

In the case of the iron ore that was used to create a hammer in the example that we mentioned earlier, sufficient gravitational force was put around the atoms constituting that piece of iron ore, for it to become an integral part of planet Earth and, a small extra reserve in case it should become detached as in the case of the hammer being taken in the air.

But, eventually, the attractive force, gravity, between the Earth and that pierce of iron ore becomes too separated and the link is lost. Then that piece of iron ore (or a hammer) would float in space having lost all its connection to its home planet Earth.

We should also state that it will never be attracted to anything – a passing asteroid, a UFO or whatever – as the attractive force only applies to Earth.

But we notice, if we look at our galaxy, a number of planets, most of them orbiting the Sun.

We need to describe the forces keeping them all in place.

As we have mentioned, each and every molecule that constitutes each and every atom has a unique force connected to it that "tells" it to what object, person, planet, rock, animal, it is destined to assist or become associated with.

This is an extraordinary statement to make and we do understand that there will be many unable to accept this.

However, as the phrase goes, we will say that this is physics and, long years into the future, man will evolve and develop instruments capable of working in both physical and spiritual dimensions (there is only spiritual in the sense of non-physical) so there will be a joining of the two aspects and instruments capable of quantifying such matters will be developed.

Then what we tell you now will become scientific fact.

For the moment, accept, if you can, what we tell you so that we can take our explanations on.

We were discussing the sun and the various planets.

Now, if we step back and look at all the life forms on planet Earth and consider the mass of atoms, each one exclusively linked to each one of those life forms and, within each atom, a series of molecules, each one also exclusively designed to assist each and every life form, we can see that planet Earth has a myriad of disparate forces floating about or contained in association with all these life forms.

So, that would imply that the planet Earth would not have a unique identity but would be the result of this hodge podge of countless identities.

But we have a suspicion that, in order for planet Earth to be held in the grip of the sun through gravity, a unique force should be emitted either by the sun or by the Earth or by both to create that bond.

This is exactly what happens.

The Earth, like all things, is alive – that is all there is in existence (life) – and so it, too, like all things is made of atoms each atom containing molecules and each one of these atoms has a stamp that tells it that it is destined to be part of the planet Earth.

Planet Earth is huge in relation to any other object living on or in it and so the number of atoms that contain the stamp corresponding to Earth is much greater than the number of atoms that constitute even the largest of creatures.

So, we have planet Earth glowing (if we can thus describe) with its own unique frequency, broadcasting out into space its signature thanks to its gravitational signal.

This signature is largely composed of weak gravity although we will state that like all things, including the imaginary ball we mentioned earlier, there is a strong gravitational field surrounding the Earth attempting to keep its integrity complete.

It is this gravitational force field that stops rocks from flying off into space as the planet dashes around the sun.

Have you ever thought about the speed that the Earth is hurtling through space?

If you take the trouble to measure how far the planet Earth is from the sun and calculate the distance it travels in a year to complete its orbit of the sun and translate that into speed, you would find it an astonishing velocity.

Add to that, that the planet is also spinning and connect that to your calculations you would see that it is a miracle that anything could remain on the surface and not be projected into space.

It is thanks to gravity that we all remain here.

At the risk of ruining what seems a good story we must, for the sake of honesty, remind you that this is all illusion and occurs just in collective imagination but we will also state that, from our present prospective it all seems real and, if you wanted, you could calculate the speed you are hurtling around the planet and through space.

We will also state that the sun is not stationary but is itself, orbiting a larger body that has not yet been discovered by science, and all that is, itself orbiting even larger bodies endlessly into the cosmos.

But, there is no point in discussing any of this at this time because most of humanity is not ready to discuss such topics.

It is all outside of any general consideration and is only mentioned for you relatively few sufficiently open-minded enough to accept such possibilities.

It will be many long years before science catches up with you but it is important that you, who read these books and can accept what we tell you, act as the vanguard for future humanity who will, one day, catch up and accept that which today they reject.

It is you who project this acceptance into the Akashic Record that creates the pocket of information that others will connect with and we thank you for your open mindedness.

Without perhaps realizing it, by accepting this wisdom you are aiding future humanity, sowing the seeds so as this information blossoms, people will be able to accept it.

This first step – sowing the seeds in the Akashic Record – is essential for future humanity to accept and to grow both in wisdom and in spirituality.

So, we send our sincere thanks to you all who can accept this information: for far too long has progress been retarded by those who have banned such information and done their utmost to suppress any and all relations by those who, through various means, were able to see and to understand such concepts as we, once again, present to you.

Nothing is new and all we tell you in these books and publications has been revealed over and over again. Presented in ways that were understandable to the peoples of those times and of the countries in which the sages, selected to reveal that information, lived.

As we have mentioned before, we hope that thanks to modern methods of communication this information will remain in public until it is accepted by all good minded people and, eventually taught in schools and universities replacing the false teachings that are currently being disseminated.

So, let us return to planet Earth and its gravitational connection to its parent body, the Sun.

Now, the sun is an extraordinary object, far more complex and marvelous than scientists tell us.

32

Once again, it is negative and limited minded people who have either ignored many aspects of the sun or who have deliberately suppressed any spiritual aspect of it.

We have stated many times that God is light – star light – and the sun is a star.
We tend, as it is relatively close to us compared to other stars, to ignore the fact that it is a star but the truth is that it is our nearest physical connection to what we might refer to as God.
Of course, we have mentioned God many times and suggested that he (it) lives in a nowhere place removed from any dimension and have given the impression that he is a purely spiritual "being". This is, of course true but, as with many things, is not the whole truth.

God is pure light and light is vibration.
If the frequency of the sun could be measured it would, indeed, be found to vibrate and thus cause light.
The apparent intense heat generated by the sun is actually an illusion created by scientists who suppose that, because the air around our planet vibrates in harmony with the frequency of the sun and that vibration creates warmth, rather like in a microwave oven, that the sun is incredibly hot. This is not the case.
The sun is a form of portal generated by Archangels in order to permit life to exist on Earth.
It is not the moment to comment on where the other end of that portal is connected as that is a subject unto itself so, suffice to say, the light we see from what we refer to as the sun is projecting from a portal.
It has been noted that, from time to time, flying craft appear from the sun and can remain in orbit close to the sun.
People question how such craft can withstand such intense heat but that is because most people have no concept that the sun does not project heat, it projects light – vibration – and the sun is actually quite cool.

However, our interest is to find how and why this portal should keep a relatively large number of diverse planets in a gravitational grip.

There is a relationship between light (vibration) and gravity and the two, gravity and vibration, are closely connected and one is a reflection of the other.
If this is true, the vibration from the sun acts up on the various planets and causes them to vibrate in harmony with the vibrations of the sun.

Now, we can immediately see that we have created a problem for ourselves because we have stated earlier that each and every planet has its own, unique, frequency and this is true, but now we are saying that the frequency of the sun plays a part in creating gravity. Let us try to explain.

It all starts with God – or rather the Archangels who actually create everything.
As we have said, in order for life to exist, there must be order.

There would be no point in life essences just floating aimlessly in a void so the concept of gravity was created as a means of putting order in life.

This has resulted, as we have already stated in the case of planet Earth being constructed of molecules held inside a coating called atoms, these atoms creating a body called Earth and that body's integrity being maintained by gravity and also that, to keep that body (Earth) in orbit around the sun, a weak form of gravity is projected towards the sun to act as an elastic band allowing the planet Earth to swing around somewhat but, nevertheless, held in a grip so that it cannot wander off into the cosmos. That elastic grip is termed an ellipse.

We hope that you can understand this, at least in principle.

However, there is more to gravity than we might have touched on but not really explained.

We have mentioned the law of mutual attraction, like attracting like. This, as the words imply, means that two similar essences are attracted to each other which also implies that the attractive force must work in both directions simultaneously.

So, we suggest to you that the Earth is projecting a gravitational field (force) out towards the sun but the sun is also doing the same, projecting a gravitational force towards the Earth.

Now, this concept is further complicated by the fact that we said that the sun is a portal which can be imagined as a trumpet and there is some "musician" on the other end of the trumpet playing a tune.

This is obviously a ridiculous over simplification of reality but, at the same time, it is not so far from the truth.

There is no musician blowing down the trumpet but there is the God force that is being projected down this trumpet, this tube, this portal and is projecting that force – that vibration - out into the cosmos, and one of the notes it plays corresponds to the frequency of the gravitation of Earth.

So, we hope that you can see from this childish but effective analogy that planet Earth is projecting a gravitational force towards the sun and the sun is responding by projecting an identical force towards Earth.

Both forces are vibration and the two have been described as the music of the cosmos.

We cannot hear this music but it is there acting ceaselessly between the sun and Earth according to the law of mutual attraction and these two forces hold Earth in orbit around the sun.

This music of the cosmos is being projected according to the unique frequencies of all the planets in our galaxy in exactly the same manner as that between Earth and the sun, so all the planets are held in their respective orbits.

Equally, if one were to visit other galaxies, this same process is going on between their sun(s) and the various planets orbiting those suns.

We wish also to mention that our complete galaxy also has a gravitational force field around it holding the entire galaxy together and to keep it from wandering off and colliding with any other galaxy.

Can you imagine the devastation that would be caused if two entire galaxies collided and split (detonated)?

34

However, putting that impossibility aside, we wish you to consider carefully what we have told you about gravity. Much of it has been revealed within these pages for the first time.

Now, we are aware that we have not fully explained just what gravity is because it is a spiritual force and although it is always our burning desire to explain as fully as we can all aspects of creation; there are some fundamental building blocks of life that just cannot be explained. We have approached as closely as possible the origins of gravity and told you of its connection to the law of mutual attraction and we have told you about these vibrations that the sages called "the music of the cosmos". We have told you that all is light, vibration and that all links intimately back to God.

As God is love, can it be that gravity is a form of love?

Can it be that gravity, which is so fundamentally connected to creation and, it is fair to say that, without the effects of gravity, nothing would exist is, in fact, the handmaiden of creation itself.

What else can we say to describe just what gravity is?

Science limits itself to describing its effects and stops at that.

We also have described its effects, we hope, in greater detail than most scientific treaties but we cannot actually describe the nature of gravity whilst remaining in a fairly down to Earth, scientific manner.

We feel that it is connected to God itself but cannot be sure.

So, with reluctance we stop in our investigation of gravity and return to the task in hand, which was, you remember, investigation of a strange galaxy that we have discovered.

CHAPTER 5

THE BIRTH OF LIFE

So, we launch ourselves, psychically, if not physically, towards this strange ball that we encountered at the beginning of this work.

You may remember that we took the plunge, so to speak, and we found ourselves in a sort of jelly that we now know, thanks to our investigations of gravity, to be the variety that is known as strong gravity.

From our investigations of atoms, we come to the strange conclusion that we are inside some sort of gigantic atom.

However, what we said before is that an atom is composed of a number of molecules contained within a strong magnetic or gravitational force and each atom floats in a weak gravitational force.

But we are within a strong magnetic force so we assume that we might be within a form of gigantic atom.

This might suggest that the various points of light, varying in intensity are, in fact, some sorts of molecules, according to our understanding of how atoms are constructed.

The question is, "why should these molecules shine or glow, some with considerable force and some more dimly?"

We need to investigate this phenomenon and try to find an answer.

So, we approach the nearest one until we are close enough to be influenced by its component(s). We find, much to our surprise, that we are in touch with a form of intelligence.

The light that shines from this planet sized molecule, floating in the thick gravitation force field that keeps it prisoner, separate from any other molecule, contains a prime sort of intelligence.

As we link with this object more and more we are able to discover that it contains life. Not in anyway that we would be able to dialogue with but a form of original, created life force.

Now, we cogitate on this strange event and try to understand what we are interacting with and, eventually, we come to the conclusion that we are looking at and interacting with a form of primitive life that was created before life as we know it was created.

We understand that life is light (vibration) and so we assume that the life forms that constitute the glowing spheres inside this galaxy sized atom, each one is a form of life and some have more "life" associated with them than others.

Now, this raises other questions. Why, for instance should some objects shine more brightly than others?

This does not make sense as, if it was all created at the same time, one would think that all would be at the same stage of development and thus would all shine with equal force. But clearly this is not so.

We look around this giant atom and we start to notice that there are planet sized molecules that do not really glow at all and thus remain dark and almost invisible in this strange world.

Now, we cut a long story short here and tell you the conclusions that we came to after much discussion with very advanced beings who are aware of these strange worlds.

What we are looking at is the creation of life itself. Obviously, this needs explaining.

Long, long before life as we know it to be came into our awareness, it already existed. But it existed in forms that had absolutely no connection to life as we know it. This is going to be difficult to explain so we ask you to open your minds and just let this information flow into you without trying really to analyse or comprehend because, at first it won't make much sense.

But, the truth seems to be that, just as God has always existed, so life has always existed. God and life seem to be irrevocably connected so we could say that God is life and life is God.

However, we assume that God has never altered although we have no proof of that as we cannot actually contact this force we call God, but there is evidence that life has altered, evolved, so that we can say that life as we know it today is not the same as it was countless millions of years ago.
But no matter how far we have been able to travel back in history, and some very advanced human Archangels have travelled a vast distance into the past, life in one form or another has always existed.
This may ride hard with some religious people who consider that God created life relatively recently but we must present the truth as we know it to be and apologise to anyone offended.

However, we will also say that the Biblical version of life has some truth to it, that life as we know it is a somewhat recent, in cosmological terms, creation, as the life that we are referring to in the distant past, that we are discussing, is different indeed to any life as it is presented today.
But, we repeat, life, like God, has always existed.

But let us return once more to the life that we were considering inside this galaxy sized atom in the far distant past.
We noticed that some "molecules" seemed to glow more brightly than others so logic dictated that some molecules were more advanced than others.
Therefore, we assume that life is not created in one fell swoop but created molecule by molecule.
This also defies logic. The only similar things that we can relate to today that follow a similar pattern are creatures such as ants or bees. The queen of that species creates, during her life, an endless flow of eggs, one after another, each one containing a life force and each one developing into a living, thinking entity – an ant or a bee.

So, did that concept come from what we are observing here? Would this account for the life forms being at a different stage of development?

Next, we ask ourselves, 'where is the being creating these life forms and what do these life forms develop into, if anything?'

We can only assume that God creates life so, if the life forms it creates are visible to our astral eyes, as planet sized molecules, could God be visible rather as we could see a queen ant or bee producing eggs?

But then we realize that, compared to a queen of its species, we are huge and can observe the process of creating eggs from a higher perspective than the queen, who is probably not even aware that we exist and are observing what she is doing.

We can hardly consider ourselves greater than God, so we abandon the idea of watching him producing life forms.

We must apologise for sometimes calling God it or sometimes he but we have no word in the English language to describe a being that has no relation to anything that we could relate to. We mean no offense to anyone but we do not wish to write he/she/it every time we refer to God so we use the word we think to be the most appropriate in the circumstances.

So, we do our best to observe the creation of these life forms and we notice that one by one they just appear as dark orbs.

Now, once again we must apologise for creating a sort of childish story because the truth is that what we have just said about these life forms appearing we have actually been told by human Archangels of great age and wisdom who have, themselves, observed this strange phenomenon.

But what we have told you is true.

In this galaxy sized ball of strong gravity, a vast number of planet sized spheres of energy, of life, are being created, or were long ago.

Of course, as is so often the case, this raises more questions than it answers.

We are sure that you can think of some yourself. Why should God's Archangels be creating from the one life that God himself created, a huge number of life forms? What purpose would they serve either at that time or into the future?

Once again, to cut a long story short, we were observing the beginning of all life that was, much later, put into the 8th dimension of our reality.

We have mentioned to you that God created a vast but exact number of points of life that would be used to create everything, in all dimensions and throughout all time. That exact number of points of life had to come from somewhere, and this strange galaxy sized atom is the place where those points of life were created. We realize that is takes a stretch of imagination to believe, but it is so.

One by one, these points of life were created and placed into this strange atom rather like a queen ant or bee creating the eggs for her colony.

Over just how vast a period of time it took for God and his trusted Archangels to create this vast, incalculable number of points of life we have no means of understanding.

Time, of course, doesn't really exist, except in our imaginations but, nevertheless, it must have taken an enormous period of time – in our terms – for God to create all these aspects of life.

As we have said, God created the exact numbers that he needed to create every facet of life everywhere and throughout time but it was done and everyone of them was placed in this gigantic atom. Each one floating silently in its web of gravity.

Now, we mentioned that some of these points of life glowed more brightly than others. This implies that some form of spiritual development must be going on inside each one of these molecules rather as we might observe in an ant or bee egg as it develops or, indeed, in a chicken egg as it develops into a chick.

Once again, we question what is occurring and once again we must turn to the sages for the answer.

All life is one.

Therefore, we must assume, even in those far off days and in that primordial gravitational soup – if we may thus call it – what we observe today must have a strong connection to what was occurring then.

An egg – whether it be of an ant or a bee or of a chicken, develops and the life form inside it gradually changes from a sort of liquid into the solid body of something.

But yet, we know that the points of life that exist in the 8th plane of our dimension have no form. They are just points of life without any denomination.

So, we question what these points of life might develop in to?

The answer is that they develop into God. Obviously, this needs explaining.

The basic astral shape of everything is a sphere. So, what we are observing in this galaxy sized globe is an incalculable number of spheres, each one containing the life force we know as God.

But here is yet another aspect of God that people might have difficulty in accepting.

We think of God as perfect. This must be true but that does not mean to say that the God spirit placed inside each sphere is itself total perfection.

God has curiosity and curiosity implies investigation and growth.

Therefore, God – or rather the Archangels charged by God to create all these aspects of life – pretended that he was an embryo. Thus, he pretended to be alive but that is all.

Life is light and the more aware that light is the brighter it glows. The converse is also true. Lack of awareness indicates a lack of light which is why, at first, the spheres have almost no brightness to them.

But life learns and, as it does, so it glows brighter as the power of God flows into it. It was true then and is true today. As modern humans absorb the power of God, so a light, a spiritual light emanates from their bodies and can be seen by those gifted with astral vision. The word astral implies light so any object or person who has absorbed the spiritual power of God glows with the light of God – star light. This is why angelic beings glow so brightly. They have absorbed spiritual essence and that shines forth as light.

As we observe the various aspects of life being created, one by one in this gigantic sphere we see that, one by one, as they wake up to what they are, aspects of God, and absorb that power within them, so they start to glow with the spirit of God which manifest itself as light.
Our own curiosity pushes us to investigate some of these created aspects of God.

In case we have not made this quite clear we wish to explain again what we are observing in the far distant, both in terms of dimension (as in distance from our universe) and in terms of time. We are observing creation that is taking place in an unimaginable distance from us and in unimaginable eons of time in the past.
We are observing the very moment when everything that has ever existed, is existing or will exist in any dimension or aspect of life, was created.
One way to imagine this is to consider every molecule of every atom as being created as individual living aspects of God and every one of these countless molecules are alive and sentient.
This is not exactly true but we do not wish to become bogged down in a long explanation of points of life which is a subject that has been mentioned before.

Suffice to say that not only is each atom alive but each molecule within each atom is alive and a specific number of these points of life were created and contain life.
This life is God itself, but the Archangels endowed each molecule not only with life (God), but gave each molecule the power to develop that power of God, as and when it felt ready to draw that power within it.

We don't know if you can grasp this concept so we will do a quick resumé again and apologise for labouring the point but it is of great importance and we wish you to have a solid understanding.

The single life force we refer to as God, with the assistance of Archangels, created a vast but specific number of aspects of God. These aspects originally contained very little of the power of God above the amount necessary to enable each point to be alive.
But, these points of life were endowed with the curiosity to investigate where they came from and thus drew more of the life force into them. That force caused them to glow with God's power, which is seen as light.

We hope that you can now see clearly in your minds eye this vast number of points of life, some glowing more brightly than others because one of those points of life eventually became you!
This is a startling realization to know that had you been with us watching all this creation we were observing, not only the one aspect that became you – the intelligence that is reading this book – but all the countless molecules inside all the countless atoms that create your body, your auras, your thoughts, all that, that is the totality of you and all other things, past, present, and future, were being created before your eyes.

40

Even to read about it is bizarre. Actually, to watch it unfold would have been quite amazing.

Even more amazing is that all these life forms contained in this galaxy sized atom were created one by one and each one is still around and active now.
Some are on Earth and constitute all the life that was, is and will be here on Earth, including all the auras attached to each life force, plus those creating all the planets plus all the thoughts, ideas, plans and concepts that any and all living things have created in their minds and are now contained in the Akashic Records, all of it was created at that period that we are attempting to describe to you.

We ask ourselves if it would be possible to approach one or more of these planet sized life forms and if it would be possible to stand on the surface and investigate these things. Obviously, we would do this with great caution because who amongst us has ever stood on something we call life? Who amongst us has the faintest idea of what such a thing might have in store for the temeraire adventurer?

CHAPTER 6

INTO THE UNKNOWN AGAIN

The problem with getting involved with situations like this is that all we have to go on to guide us are past experiences and any instruments that have been conceived to analyse matters that we have previously encountered.

To answer any questions as to if we do have instruments to help us in the non-physical realms, the answer is yes, we do.

After all, any physical tool, from a simple hammer to the most advanced device is thought turned into physical matter.

The tool started as a thought and that thought is stored in the Akash so, as thoughts have reality in whatever dimension they are attached to, we have all sorts of investigation tools at our disposition. We may not need a hammer but our investigation of creation has been greatly assisted by the various tools we have. Some of these tools you might be familiar with in physicality but many have not yet been suggested to you in physicality for a variety of reasons.

So, we do have tools that assist us but, in this case, we draw a blank. As far as we are aware, no one has encountered raw, basic life and so we are very cautious as we approach one of these life creations that resemble planet sized spheres.

We should say that the fact that these life forms are huge does not bother us as we have encountered, elsewhere, early creation and it has been very large. In these astral planes size has little relevance and many things start out large before being reduced in size.

One simple example would be early computers. When they were made of valves (tubes), even a fairly simple computer could be room size whereas now a motherboard of a modern computer contains a vast number of elements, transistors, capacitors, resistors, all reduced to microscopic size scarcely visible to the naked eye.

So, size does not concern us, indeed it might well be an aid.

To investigate a life form that would take an electron microscope to see would hamper us but to stand in a life form the size of a planet would, or should, be an advantage.

However, there might be danger.

As we are in a non-physical universe here, nothing can harm us physically, but we are as vulnerable as you concerning mental or emotional thoughts and experiences. Even in the astral realms we need to be circumspect about entering unknown thought areas.

So, we do the wise thing and seek advice from the human Archangels that have vast amounts of knowledge and experience in the hopes that they can enlighten us.

They inform us, much as we had suspected, that we were, indeed, observing the creation of life in what they called the relatively recent past although it must be said that this past was a very long time ago indeed.

But they went on to inform us that life has always existed and each time it follows the same pattern.

It is born, grows to maturity, to perfection and that perfection returns to God and ceases to exist. It has completed its cycle.

At that point, God starts again in another area of "nothingness" and creates a new existence.

This, apparently, has been happening forever but it is all created one at a time.

One might imagine that God, being God, could create many existences at a time but, apparently it is not so.

The existence that we are part of was started long ago, and will continue long into the future until the last life essence that we were watching being created has reached perfection and merges back to God, at which point God withdraws – all that he created disappears and God starts again.

This may all seem a bit pointless and we suppose it is if one is hoping for some mystical meaning to life above and beyond the beauty of life itself but we must accept that God has decided to create life like this and we must accept that is how it has always been and always will.

So, to repeat, what we were observing was the creation of life itself this time around.

Just how many times God (existence) has created all this we have no means of knowing.

We are told that creation (God) has always existed and so we can only accept that.

But it does not help us deciding if it is safe to step foot upon the planet sized elements of life being created in the galaxy sized atom.

We need at least two questions answered before we approach too closely one of these life forms:

1. Is it safe for us to do so, and
2. Can we do so without disturbing, polluting that life force.

The answer to both of these questions was given in the affirmative and the reason explained. We are looking at the very same life being created that we are part of so we are not inimical to it being, ourselves, part and parcel of that same life force.

It is as if we are part of the same creative force that is busy at work creating life itself and, eventually, one of these life forces will become us, long eons of time into the future and, eventually, many of these life forces will be used to created every aspect of us; physical, emotional, mental or spiritual.

Therefore, not only are we totally compatible with all these created life forms but each one of them are, themselves, compatible, interchangeable and are, in fact, aspects of the one created force we term God.

Let us, for a moment, break off from our investigation of life's creation and discuss the word "God".

Now, it is difficult to talk about God because, of course, no one understands what God is and where it came from.

We don't even really know that God exists. We just know that something creates all that is and we call that force by a variety of names including "God".

So, all we can really say is that something creates everything – or so we assume – and we call that something "God".

Some scientist claim not to believe in God, and that is understandable because we cannot explain what God is but, when asked what creates all that exists, they have to admit that they don't know.

Some beings, of a "scientific" nature try to claim that life just formed from a primordial soup of elements but cannot explain where those elements originated so that explanation is hardly satisfactory.

Some religious authorities claim that God is a judgmental being and has been described as an old man with a long white beard sitting on a cloud and condemning vast numbers of people to hell for some crime. The prime ones being a failure to accept the teachings of those religious leaders. Whilst we give everyone the freedom to think as they choose, a moment's thought would reveal some gaps in that logic especially when one points out all the different aspects of life that science is now beginning to discover.

Then again, God has been described as "existence". We understand the meaning of the word existence and do not disagree with that definition because, by implication everything exists but, somehow, the word existence feels a little light weight as we investigate the marvels of life. One feels that it is in some way by passing a full explanation.

The problem is that even the word "God" is a means of avoiding any definitions as God has a number of definitions according to the beliefs of the person writing the word.

So, all we can really say is that common sense tells us that something created life and we do not have any idea of where that something came from, if that something was, itself, created by or from something else that existed before what we refer to as God came into being but whatever it is that creates all that is, some of us call God.

We do not wish to imply any religious implication or connotation to the word God. Where we speak of God we are referring to prime creator as a simple fact. Something created everything and we refer to that something as God.

So, having been reassured that we could not harm or be harmed by approaching a life form – planet – we choose one of the darker ones as a first experience and stepped foot onto it.

Now, we are going to find difficult, words of sufficient descriptive power to explain the experience.

We first will say that light was almost entirely absent. This, of course, was not unexpected as we had already chosen one that emitted little light.

But, we noticed that although from the exterior this planet sized object seemed solid, in fact it was more like being in a liquid. This is not a totally accurate description as, in fact, what we should say is that it was more lack of solidity than the reality of liquid. This is not easy to explain and, we are sure, even more difficult to comprehend but we are floating in a something that lacks solidity but cannot really be described as liquid.

The first thing is to try to investigate what this strange matter is.

It turns out to be unformed life.

Now, on Earth, if we crack open a newly laid egg we find a liquid but this liquid can be analysed and we find that it is in part albumen. But we have a feeling that the liquid in which we are floating is this strange world and would not totally conform to anything we might find on Earth.

So, all we can say for the moment is that we are in unformed life essence.

It appears clear, like water, to our astral eyes because, don't forget we are in a non-physical place, but yet we sense that it has the potential to contain all colors eventually. These colors do not exist for the moment but we sense that propensity for them to appear one day.

No matter how much we analyse this liquid, we find no reference points in any material with which we are familiar so just have to accept that unformed life essence has this liquid form.

However, we are not satisfied with that because we are sure that we are breaking new ground in our investigation of life's origins. If we were to try to imagine the first aspect of creation, we would assume that it would have some form of solidity, even in a high astral sense, but this liquid does not conform to what we might imagine.

This is where we have, once again, to refer to the wise beings who have already seen, studied and understood the progression of life from this liquid into a solid form that can, one day, far into the future, become life as we know it whether it be animal, vegetable, mineral, or astral.

All becomes molecules which form atoms which, in turn, become some aspect of creation.

So, this liquid must, eventually, become solid even in an astral sense.

Now, we mentioned that we would be breaking new ground in trying to comprehend the nature of life and yet we mentioned that there are very advanced beings that had already understood the process. So, we are not actually the first to reach into this conundrum and pull out the answer.

So, please let us take a moment to explain, as far as we can, the nature of the Archangels to whom we refer.

We have already explained in a previous work the incredible suffering that needs to occur that transforms an already advanced "ordinary" person into a human Archangel so we will not repeat that information.

However, as you should know by now, life is endless and for those courageous people that take this final step in the long progression towards perfection, once they become Archangels they have access to other areas of knowledge above and beyond that available to lesser mortals.

We used the word mortal in its sense, not of being physical but of being less than God itself.

There is an aspect of life that we will just mention to try to explain how we are able to obtain advanced information although it would be quite impossible for anyone less than an Archangel to access this area of information.

We have said that the Akashic Record is the area in which all information, since the dawns of time, is stored. This is so, but this is an aspect of the Akashic Record that is difficult to comprehend.

The Akashic Record has been called a living library and this is true.

Every aspect of every event that has occurred since what we might refer to as existence, God and the Archangels, who work for God producing life, first created life as we have explained it in previous works.

So, we are going back to the moment when the eight dimensions were created.

We might consider that moment as the beginning of existence as we might understand it.

All of that is stored in the Akashic Record and, for those able to access those areas and comprehend what they see, it is readily accessible.

However, as we are trying to explain in this book, creation started long before the creation of the eight dimensions.

This is the time that we are investigating now.

So, we have two aspects to what we might call "modern times".

We have that vast amount of time since the eight dimensions were created that has developed into our times and then we have the long period of time when life itself, this time around was created – the time that we are investigating.

The Akashic Record would, of course, record this time but, because it deals with creation before the introduction of the eight dimensions, this aspect of Akashic Record is separate and not readily available to us.

One way to imagine it would be to consider an important library today which would have many books available to public gaze and a reserve or restricted section only available to a select few.

This select few would be the human Archangels who have progressed to the point that they are almost beyond the point of being contacted by us.

These Archangels are no longer directly concerned with educating the public as we are which is why some of the information they have at their disposal they do not always share with us.

They have different tasks, different priorities which occupy them.

Thus, they are able to open doors into areas of God's creation which would remain closed to us but for the knowledge of these human Archangels.

We were discussing this liquid which formed the centre of these planet sized molecules.

We know two things about these molecules – three if we take into account the thick gravity which surrounds each molecule. But in the interior, we know that there is thin gravity and also "life", whatever that enigmatic substance is.

But our immediate problem is how to differentiate between gravity and life?

Now, this is where the knowledge imported by the human Archangels we consulted comes in invaluable for they have revealed to our astonished minds a secret concerning life. It seems that life and gravity are intricately entwined to the point that we might consider them to be one and the same.

Obviously, among all the improbable information we have so far reported to you, this is the most outlandish, and we do appreciate you rejecting utterly this concept. If it were not for the fact that we trust completely these wise and noble beings – human Archangels – we would have instantly rejected such an unbelievable notion. But we asked them to explain.

It appears that life is a natural process created by a simple spiritual law that we have mentioned many times before and without realizing it's full implication: the law of mutual attraction, like attracts like.

We know some of the implications of this law as we are sure you do also. We are all attracted to people and concepts that correspond to our own personalities and our own interests.
We have also talked at some length about everything, everyone, and every spot in the multiverse having a unique frequency.
We have mentioned that of all of the atoms in the universe, only the ones that have your particular frequency are attracted to you, all other atoms remaining unattracted to you awaiting the moment when they would be drawn to something and someone having the same frequency.
We have briefly mentioned the sun blasting from its portal a number of certain frequencies, each one corresponding to the unique frequency of any planet which, in term, radiates a certain unique frequency and it is this frequency that holds the planets in orbit around the sun. We referred to it as the music of the cosmos.
So, we realize that frequencies (vibrations) are themselves closely connected to gravity.

Now we start to put two and two together and hope to unravel the concept, the mystery, of life in its most basic form.

If it is true that the law of mutual attraction is the motivating force for life and this law needs frequencies in order to manifest itself, it follows that gravity creates, by way of the law of mutual attraction, life.
Life, it appears, is formed as matter is formed due to this basic law of mutual attraction and, to draw things together, unique vibrations are employed and to hold them together gravity is used.

Can you comprehend this amazing truth? Life, even though we think that it is created by God is, in practical, down to Earth terms, the result of molecules drawn together and glued together by gravity and the result is basic life. Life without any form, knowledge or destination, but life nevertheless.
Of course, as each life force is given a stamp – a logos – to tell it what it is, it progresses and, through the experience of whatever form it chooses to become, becomes almost unrecognizable compared to the basic life form it started out as.

We, in this planet sized molecule, were actually inside basic life, a mixture of gravity and vibration, plus the law of mutual attraction.

This, of course, for those who expected life to be of a much more esoteric nature might be disappointed to find that life is no more than a vibration held together by gravity.

Perhaps this is what the Bible was trying to tell us in the statement, "In the beginning was the word and the word was with God and the word was God." John 1:1

Could it be that "the word" mentioned was a way of explaining to simple people of that time that life is vibration?

We cannot comment on the meaning that was implied by the word "word", but we can assure you that life is a natural process brought about by like attracting like and it vibrates and is held together by gravity.

However, we who were now inside this liquid realized that the liquid was weak gravity although we felt no vibration.

We did, however, notice that, as we advanced, this liquid, this weak gravity, moved away from us as we progressed so that we never touched it and were always in a sort of bubble of nothingness.

Of course, the reason for this is obvious. This gravity was vibrating at its own unique frequency while we also were vibrating at our unique frequencies and so the gravity, in this molecule, found our frequencies to be incompatible to its and so the converse to the law of mutual attraction came into action – the law of mutual rejection.

To preserve its integrity, it rejected our frequencies and left us in a bubble of emptiness, except for our own frequencies, which it sensed and rejected.

Can you imagine what it feels like to be in a place that is actually basic, raw life but there is nothing to see, not much to feel only a weak gravitational force that we know to be vibrating? Every particle of our being cries out for a more concrete evidence to demonstrate that life is a more tangible product than just gravity vibrating. It took quite a while for us to be able to accept this strange fact – that the most important aspect of existence, life itself, is no more than weak gravity vibrating inside a molecule, no matter how large or small it appears to be.

But we eventually realize that God's Archangels have almost miraculous methods of constructing what we might term to be existence and if anything was too complicated, there is always the chance that something might go wrong and so they discovered this very simple way of putting together the most important aspect of existence, life itself, in the simplest way possible.

For those who may not have fully comprehended what life is we explain again. It is a combination of a few simple facts: The spiritual law of mutual attraction placed inside a sphere of weak gravity with a coating of strong gravity surrounding the sphere and the weak gravity is then made to vibrate at a frequency, each sphere having its own unique frequency. That then becomes life. How and why, we must confess we do not really know because it is impossible to emulate this in a laboratory. We know that some biologists claim to have manufactured basic life in test tubes using a soup of amino acids etc., but they fail to realize that those very amino acids contain life already – everything being alive – and they are merely propagating that life.

To create life from nothing, only gravity, is not in the purview of any living being in any domain. It is only the God force in conjunction with his Archangels that know how to perform the trick. Many have tried and they all have failed.

So, we question as to whether there is more than just a spiritual law, gravity and vibration to life but even our most extensive research over a long period of time has not revealed any previously hidden factor that transforms these basic facts into life in an almost alchemical fashion.

It does appear, indeed, that the combination of these simple ingredients, the law of mutual attraction in combination with weak gravity which is made to vibrate does create basic life.

And yet it is impossible to emulate the process.

So, we must leave the process there and continue with our explorations.

We cover all of this planet sized molecule and discover nothing more.

We cannot, in all honesty, say that we detect any actual life on this sphere. It is dark and silent. There is no movement, no spark of life and nothing to demonstrate to our senses that it is alive.

It is only assurance by the immensely wise human Archangels that this type of molecule is the beginning of basic life that assures us that it is alive. It may well be alive but it is barely so.

Let us now turn our attention to another sphere, another molecule of life in this galaxy sized atom that appears much more promising, much more glowing with life.

We approach one of the brighter spheres and plunge through the thick outer coating of strong gravity into the mass of weak gravity inside.

Now this form of gravity is exactly the same as the previous in terms of its consistency and in terms of the fact that it shied away from us as we traversed it but this gravity glowed with light.

The basic color was pure white but we noticed that, from time to time, that white light would change into beautiful pale, pastel colors, blue, red (or pink), green and various other colors.

This indicated to us a more developed aspect of life.

We know that pure white light is associated with the God force and we also know that colors are associated with emotions. So, we conclude that the God force – whatever that is – is more developed in this sphere and it also has the beginnings of emotions.

This is both to be expected and is also somewhat surprising.

It is surprising in that we expected basic life force to be without emotions and that emotion would develop more in the type of life as we know it and not in this far off time and galaxy. But clearly, if we have read these astral colors correctly, the beginnings of emotion were placed here.

We question why this is so and to what degree would emotion develop in these strange life forms?

Indeed, we go on to query what type of emotion could possibly develop in this rather static life essence as it seems to be totally without the possibility of obtaining any tangible form of experience that could provoke any type of emotional reaction.

Once again, we turn to our human Archangels to provide the answers that are actually quite obvious when we are told.

We mentioned earlier that life has always existed and that what we are observing in the creation of this basic life and what we experience in our lives has been repeated over and over again.

We also mentioned that, when the last of the created life forms progress to perfection it at last merges with God at which point the whole thing disappears and God starts again in another area of nothingness.

But, of course, the one thing that does carry on without pause is God himself.

He has gained in wisdom from each creation and so we may assume that God has attracted to himself immense knowledge and wisdom.

Therefore, we assume that God, or rather his Archangels, are able to pass some of that wisdom to these life forms as they develop and, as all knowledge is connected to God in one way or another, we see it as a spiritual light which is why some of these orbs glow with a degree of whiteness.

We also assume, from the colors that we see that these life forms have the beginnings of emotion stirring within them.

Can we work out why and how these spheres of basic life develop?

We have already given the answer elsewhere but will repeat it here.

This force we call God – which we notice is not just life – is responsible for the creation of life. God is outside of creation.

But the aim of God is always one and the same. It creates life, pushes that life to grow to immense power and wisdom and then, finally, it reabsorbs that life, disappears and restarts again, endlessly.

It is a strange concept to create something, push it to grow and then reabsorb all that knowledge and repeat that process endlessly but it is so.

Therefore, we are watching the beginnings of life being created that will eventually develop into all the life that we are currently living.

So, from that barely alive life force that we observed and described earlier, God's Archangels gently push the beginnings of knowledge into it and it begins to stir and become more alive.

Eventually, it becomes as we see the molecule that we are studying now. Not really a conscient being as we would know it, but at least conscient that it is alive and has the beginnings of emotions (desires) awake also.

At this point it is ready to take the next step and move to the 8th dimension of the existence that we have described in the book about Auras.

So, what we have been observing in this strange galaxy sized object is the kindergarten, the nursery for life to be born and to grow to the stage that it can join in the creation of life in all the dimensions and glory that we described in the last book.

But our investigation of this kindergarten galaxy is not yet finished. We have other areas to investigate to complete the story. What we have so far described is only a part of this story.

CHAPTER 7

INTO THE HEART OF THE MYSTERY

We decide to linger in this more awake molecule because our curiosity is not only peaked by the startling discovery of what life is but we thought that we might be able to pick up a few tips as to the nature of consciousness, emotion, and any other attributes of life that we might observe. The problem, if we observe any more advanced life form in our dimensions, is that basic attributes are so over ridden by more advanced attributes that it becomes very difficult to dive back to basics, to tell the wheat from the chaff, so to speak. But here we recognise a golden opportunity to observe and, we hope, to quantify the basic properties of consciousness and its various offshoots.

We remind you once again that life as we observe it, if we strip away all the illusion, is just consciousness.
Nothing in a material sense actually exists, although, through imagination it seems to, and, as we have said before, if we liken existence to an onion and strip back the layers we arrive at nothing. Actually, the example of an onion is a very apt one, if not the most pleasant life form to examine!

An onion is a solid object, a vegetable, as we are sure you know. They are very valuable and are used not only to flavour and to thicken many dishes, but contain a number of vitamins, proteins, and other elements that help keep the physical body healthy.
But in the way we intend to regard it, it is not its culinary and health properties that interest us, it is its form.
Some onions are quite small and some fairly large but the important aspect, from the point of view of this discussion, is that it grows in layers, a large number of coverings growing on top of each other and, on the outside, a protective skin that keeps the onion whole and protects it from attack by invasive creatures and by inclement weather.
So, it arrives on our kitchen table in good – we hope – condition.
So, we take off the brown protective coating and the onion is revealed.
Now, this is the interesting part, from the point of view under discussion. If we peel off the layers, one at a time, we eventually get to the heart which we find to be just a sort of compressed leaf or two. In other words, we have in the onion basket a number of onions, each one obviously solid and have, or had at one stage, the power to grow but when we take off the layers there is no obvious sign of this life force that told the onion that, not only it was alive when it was still a seed, but that it was going to grow into an onion, of which we might add there are a number of varieties.
So, something told the seed that it was going to be an onion and told it what type of onion it was going to be. But, when we examine the layers of onion as they lie on the kitchen table, apart from being able to assess the various vitamin properties the skins or layers contain, there is no obvious instructions within it to inform it of its destiny.

We know this to be consciousness and we have discussed this at various times and in various talks and publications.

Consciousness is invisible. It is not a solid object in any dimension and can only be guessed at. No one can prove that consciousness exists and yet something must exist that tells our long-suffering onion what it is going to become.

But what else does the onion know?

Does it, for example know that it is going to become an onion?

We can understand that it might know that it is alive but does it know what it is? Is it conscient enough to know that?

Does it know that it is growing on planet Earth?

Does it know that its function is largely to help humans and/or the very few animals that eat onions?

We could ask questions like that for a long time and each question takes us back to trying to determine the level of awareness, of consciousness, of our onion.

The same would apply to every object in existence from a grain of sand to our entire galaxy.

How much are things aware?

What is their level of consciousness?

We hope by examining the basic life forms in this pre-worldly (in our terms) galaxy we might find some answers.

But the problem is, to return to us floating in weak gravity within this planet sized molecule, observing both the white light and the flashes of beautiful pastel colored lights, that there is nothing that we can hook on to, to explain just what consciousness is. We see light as if the whole planet was lit by a sun and we see flashes of color as if someone was flickering a series of colored projectors on and off and yet our intelligence tells us that this molecule is more consciousness that the previous one that remained dark and inert.

So, once more we are stumped. We must return to our Archangelic mentors and seek their advice.

Before we do that, might we just remind you that we have been assured that we are observing an event in the distant past that has ultimately resulted in the total multiverse that we now live in.

Each and every aspect of life within this galaxy sized object will constitute each and every molecule that will end up in each and every atom and each one of these planet sized molecules is alive thanks to the very strange event, The Law of Mutual Attraction, creating gravity and that gravity vibrating, each one to a unique frequency.

That is about the sum total of what we have been told or have deduced from our visit so far.

We are observing the creation of all life in all of our galaxy and in all the other galaxies this time around, for this process has been repeated endlessly, over and over again.

We ask the Archangels how this consciousness progresses.

What they tell us is fairly obvious once we have been put on the right track.

The only thing that exists, really, is this thing we refer to as God although, we repeat once again, we are not putting any spiritual or religious connotation on the word God. We refer to the prime, eternal creator.

52

All life, as we have mentioned, comes and goes and the only permanent common denominator throughout all time is the creative force that can be given any name that anyone chooses but that we refer to as God.

God, it seems not only creates life – in his image – but creates a couple of other things. One of them is curiosity, the desire to learn and develop and, to do this, he deemed it necessary to place in association with life which, we remind you is a fairly automatic creation, consciousness.

Now, it must be obvious that life, although it is quite a simple process once we understand how it works, is not quite as accidental as it seems and some have described it.

It must be a deliberate act and we can almost certainly turn to God's trusted allies and servants, the Archangels, to have come up with the simple concept of using the law of mutual attraction to draw gravity together and make that vibrate and thus we have basic life.

Of course, at the base of life is this spiritual – in the sense both of non-physical and also in the sense of being positive – law and we must ask where did this law come from?

This is where we must use our common sense and intelligence and try to imagine how such a thing could have been invented. Apparently, it is true that God and creation, existence if you will, has always been.

Now, no one either carnate nor incarnate can imagine the use of the word "always" in terms of time.

We would find it quite impossible to imagine the amount of time that would pass between the beginning of the creation of the event that we are studying now, onwards into the time of the creation of the 8 dimensions until the moment that the last person, object or thing itself reaches perfection, moulds with this God force and the whole lot disappears. Such a vast amount of time would be quite impossible to imagine.

But if we multiply that by the endless number of times that this process has been repeated, we realize that it would be quite impossible to understand the meaning of the word "always" in this concept.

Indeed, as it has been said that time is an illusion, we wonder if there is not just the "now" moment and so "always" implies "now"?

However, that question we will leave for another day.

Assuming that this creation/destruction process has been going on forever and assuming that God grows in wisdom each time, can we not look back a long way and infer that there might have been a time when God and/or the Archangels were not quite as knowing as they are today?

In other words, at what stage in this endless series of creations and eliminations did God and/or the Archangels stumble across how to create life as we know it now?

At what point were emotions introduced and at what point was consciousness introduced?

Did God always know about these things and did the Archangels always know how to create the conditions for life, emotions, and consciousness?

Can we possibly answer these questions and yet it would be educational to be able to find out?

This is where we need to explain an aspect of time/space that has possibly never, or very seldom, ever been discussed in public.

It is possible to group time and space into a single moment and all of the long history going back over vast eons of time can be examined as if it was now.

We are aware that we have already mentioned that there is only the now moment and that is true. But we are talking about a different aspect of "now".

We need to try to explain that consciousness is all that exists but consciousness has never really been understood.

Most people have the impression that we are all consciousness.

This, obviously, is true or you would not be reading this book, as we have stated before.

Then there are those that can recognise that all sentient life is able to share consciousness. This is more difficult because it implies that, if this were so, we would all be able to share our thoughts, yet how many of us can really do this?

Certainly, telepathy is possible to learn but how many people are aware of what every person on the face of the planet Earth is thinking at this precise moment? It seems ridiculous even to imagine that it would be possible for any one person to be able to link with each and every other person on the face of the Earth and know what they are thinking?

And yet this is what universal consciousness implies.

And then let us take it on even further.

Imagine that it would be possible to link with the minds and thoughts of any and all people who have lived in the past, are alive now and will be in the future. Imagine that you could link with all those who live in other dimensions as well. This would be true cosmic consciousness.

Well, that is only the beginning of the sort of consciousness that we are suggesting is possible.

It is possible to link with every aspect of life throughout time because all is one and all is now.

But we can take the concept back even further and we are going to say something that surely will sound like science fiction gone crazy – but it is the truth.

It is possible not only to link with every being, creature, plant, or mineral on the face of the Earth but it can be done throughout all time and in all dimensions and, further, we can take that connection back, and back beyond this creation into and beyond all the creations endlessly into the past through the simple fact that all is one.

What you are, everything is, so there is no aspect of life – of consciousness, anywhere that is not available to you or us as all is one and time is one.

So, this has enabled us to investigate the word "always" that we mentioned in terms of existence.

Now, obviously, to achieve this remarkable feat of stretching the mind backwards and forwards and ever outwards is not available to all – yet.

It is only the purview of the most advanced Archangels and they have confided something to us concerning the never-ending construction/destruction of the life that we mentioned earlier.

We implied that life (existence) had always been and that it would always carry on. This is both true, apparently, and not true.

We have been told that this amazing creation/destruction of life going endlessly back and forth in time is all an illusion. None of it exists.

There is no creation. There is no destruction but there is something called consciousness. We will discuss consciousness a little later and we must tell you the truth that we hesitated a long time before mentioning this because, although we have implied already that everything is illusion we wanted – and still intend – to explain how you would see creation if you were to visit it and this is how it will be taught in schools in the future.

But we are obliged to tell you the truth and the truth is that there is nothing. No time, no space, nothing except for one consciousness.

All the rest has been created by you and us and the Archangels and the interdimensional beings you call aliens and so on.

All creating illusion for one reason or another, for one agenda or another.

The plain, unadorned truth is that there is nothing at all; no space – no lack of space – no concept of space – no time, no gravity, nothing at all except for this one, thankfully sempiternal concept, consciousness.

It is this consciousness that allows all the imaginary stuff to appear. It is consciousness that enables you to appear to exist and everyone else and everything else and enables imagination to create all the scenarios to appear that make life.

Consciousness is existence.

That is all that exists but it would be absolutely pointless if we all disappeared and there was just this one consciousness floating in nothing.

That is why the Archangels, who do exist but are so closely related to and connected to this force we call God, decided to create also the whole scenario that we have been attempting to describe to you and that you have been living for long ages and will continue to do for long ages into the future.

But it is important in order to understand the word "always" used in connection to life that the whole of existence as we can explore it is all illusion.

Because, in fact, always is now.

There is no "always"

How can we explain this? Perhaps one way would be to imagine a gramophone replaying endlessly the same note. Perhaps we could imagine an engine idling, turning over and over its crankshaft and its valves going up and down but the vehicle going nowhere because there is nowhere to go.

However we imagine it, this incredibly long process called life follows exactly the same process as does all life: birth, growth, decline, death (disappearance).

So, having explained that all is illusion and having explained that we must accept that we need to have some form of reality let us state that "always" is an illusion and the endless galaxy concept is just the same process of birth of the galaxy, growth, decline and death followed by an imaginary repeat of that long process, repeated over and over again.

However, even this is not true, although, if scientists could explore the far distant past they would "see" this long process stretching as far back as is possible to imagine but, in fact, it all happens just once and that is all.

It is the fact that consciousness is eternal and the "now" moment is also eternal that enables us to imagine that life has always existed and always will and, indeed, it will, but it will always exist because (a) all is illusion so anything can be created and/or imagined and (b) there is only the "now" moment so life will always continue as long as "now" continues.

So, we hope that you can see that it would be futile just to tell you that nothing exists and therefore there is nothing to explore, nothing to write about, nothing to discuss because even we do not exist when, as we open our eyes we see nothing but life. We see, just on Earth, all the planets, trees, birds, animals, people, houses and so on.

We see Archeologists exploring the past and we see mathematicians attempting to explain all sorts of things with their formulae.

In fact, it is obvious that we live in a "real" world and we can assure you from our somewhat more elevated position that your life and your education will continue endlessly into the future.

Thus, in our world, the past, present, and future are very real and it is our job to describe to you the various aspects of life as they appear to our senses.

The object of the previous description of the illusory nature of life was to explain the simple fact that "always" has no meaning and the whole process that we have been attempting to describe to you in this book, the others and all that we hope to give you in the future concerning the fact that life has "always" existed is to help you to understand that, if it happens at all, it happens just once and the concept of "always" is illusion – there is just the "now" moment.

Perhaps we need to continue on this subject for a bit longer and forestall any questions. For instance, we can imagine a day when all life reaches perfection and disappears into the God force and, having reached the end of its mission life disappears.

We have stated that God starts again in another area and repeats the process of birth, growth, decline and disappearance again.

But now we have explained that this is not so because, as there is only the "now" moment, what happens when perfection comes and life disappears?

We are going to try to explain an aspect of this illusionary, galaxy (life) that will also be rather difficult to accept.

Just as there is only consciousness and there is nothing else and just as the Archangels helped us all to create this amazing world we appear to live in, nothing can disappear.

Once the death part of the life cycle of the galaxy is reached and all disappears, so it all starts again and you will be born again.

The only image that we can present is the Phoenix rising from the ashes.

Indeed, that mythical bird was chosen to describe the very phenomenon that we have attempted to describe to you.

Very wise people, long ago, were aware that life was cyclical, and repeated itself endlessly and so, because a bird able to fly, was considered close to heaven, invented the concept of the Phoenix, which is born, matures, declines and disappears – in his case by bursting into flames – only to be reborn from the ashes of his previous existence and to repeat his life cycle again – endlessly.

It is a very apt analogy of life because the Phoenix was considered to be a very beautiful bird, and life should be beautiful, and the Phoenix had mystical powers – which you and we all have when we bother to develop them.

But you will notice that the Phoenix does not appear to grow in wisdom, it stays much as it was the last time around.

But, we can, to a certain extent, benefit from the past event – we can't call it reincarnation – because, in fact it is all illusion and is not really happening.

Reincarnation, even over such a vast time scale as we are describing from the birth of the galaxy to its extinction would have no real meaning as we all just start again.

If it were real, it would be just another revolution of a wheel, which really does not correspond to reincarnation.

We labor this point somewhat because we know that many people would like to believe in reincarnation and it is a falsehood and we do not want people to use the reincarnation of life as an "ah ha" moment and say that it is reincarnation.

Imagine it more as another revolution of the wheel.

So, we move on to the subject of this book which is to investigate the creation of life in this kindergarten galaxy, the birthplace of life, we will consider it as real because, if you could explore the astral features of the galaxy as the Archangels have, you could investigate this strange place for yourself.

Now, if you remember we were inside a molecule that was somewhat advanced and discovered that it contained white light and also some colored lights.

We discovered that this was the beginning of consciousness.

But the question that we must pose ourselves is this. We know that, eventually, a transfer will be made to the 8th dimension of the astral dimensions of our galaxy and we would like to know the details of when and how this is achieved and what would happen to this kindergarten galaxy once the last element has been transferred?

We are not the wisest beings in heaven and so we must, more and more, rely on information given to us by these very wise Archangels.

But, if we may, before we progress to tell you what they told us, may we remind you that they have access to what we might term the "restricted section" of the Akashic Record.

Now, at the risk of annoying those who would like us to continue at once with the tale we are attempting to unfold, may we take a moment to explain why this is a "restricted section" of the Akash and what information it contains.

As you may know, the Akashic Record contains the entire memory, as a sort of recording, of every being that has ever lived in our galaxy – this time around – every aspect of every thought and contains links to the other people, animals, plants, and events that anyone person has come into contact with.

Further, all information that has ever come from the mind of man is also recorded. This means, strangely enough, that every letter you have written or received, every shopping list, every comment you might have made on the internet, or received, every conversation you have had, every piece of work you have ever done throughout your working life, every book written, every painting ever made – absolutely everything is recorded in the Akashic Record and all that information is available to anyone that has the ability to enter the Akashic Record.

It is just as well that spies never take the trouble to enter the Akash because all the secrets of any and all governments are recorded there also!
There is never a moment of history that is not recorded.
Now why should this be and how is it done?

Some people have imagined that it is a vast underground cavern complete with a librarian and claim to have visited the area. This is laughable and is just childish imagination.
The simple truth, as we have said, that all that exists is consciousness.
Now, consciousness is eternal and there is just one. Therefore, it becomes a storehouse for all information.
So, when we are entering the Akashic Record, quite simply, we are entering the conscious memory of everything.
Now, as you can imagine, even though these memories are recorded and catalogued according to the unique frequency of every person and everything, unless you know the unique frequency of the person, animal, plant, or mineral you are looking for, it is not easy to find one's way about in the Akash. It is the veritable needle in the haystack problem.
We, of course, are able to navigate our way through the Akash without too much difficulty and are able to retrieve the information we require.
As we have said before, that is how these books and the other information is retrieved.
We decide which book we wish to transfer to you, books that have already been written by wise beings, sometimes alone and sometimes in collaboration with others, because these books are stored in the Akash.
Once we have located the book we required, we make the telepathic link with the instrument incarnate and transfer the information to him.
Sometimes we include comments we wish to make but, by and large, the books are transferred verbatim into the mind of the person incarnate, who writes it all down and it finishes up at your disposal.

So, after much hopping around and discussing other matters not directly related to the subject matter but which we hope you find both interesting and educational, we return to discussing consciousness and how it affects the world we are examining.
We were looking at the lights inside the planet sized molecule and wondering, among other aspects, at what point it would be considered sentient enough to be transferred to our galaxy and how all that would unfold.
Well, it turns out that the transfer process it quite natural.
This galaxy sized atom as we called it, is emitting a frequency as does everything else and that frequency corresponds to the frequency of the 8th dimension in our galaxy. So,

our old friend the Law of Mutual Attraction is at work trying to bridge the gap between this kindergarten element and the 8th dimension of our reality.

However, this Law of Mutual Attraction is also a form of gravity rather like the poles of a magnet, one end connected to this kindergarten atom and the other end connected to our galaxy.

But like a magnet, in order for it to be able to draw the two worlds together, both ends of the magnet have to be of sufficient strength. Now we are perfectly well aware that this is not a correct description of a magnet. We are using it to describe the attractive forces that will draw the two worlds together to enable the embryo life forces to transfer safely to their new home in the 8th dimension.

The power emanating from the kindergarten galaxy is dependant on the degree of consciousness – of life – of each and every molecule and so, to cut a long story short, this level of power is not reached until all the countless life essences contained with the kindergarten galaxy have all reached the point that transference is possible.

We remind you, once again, that this kindergarten galaxy will ultimately contain all the life forces that will enable life in all areas of existence to be manifest.

We could not imagine such a number, but they will ultimately be produced and will all need to grow in awareness to a certain point before sufficient power will be generated that will enable the two existences – our galaxy, or rather the 8th dimension of it, and the kindergarten galaxy – to draw close to each other and the transfer made.

The actual methodology of that transfer is quite simple but will not be described as it uses a technique that could be abused by evil people.

There are a few concepts that we prefer not to talk about because, on Earth or in the interdimensional regions, there does contain some people of less that good intent and we prefer not to give these people obvious access to weapons.

Some completely harmless and beneficial technologies can be abused and this transfer technique is one of them.

Suffice to say that, once all the countless life forces in the kindergarten galaxy reach sufficient maturity, the transfer is made and these young life forces now find themselves in the 8th dimension and will follow the course of action described in the other books that will result in them becoming me and you and all things.

The kindergarten galaxy, now having served its purpose and being bereft of any and all life forms, simply dissolves back into the basic gravitational forces from which it was made and effectively disappears. It has served its purpose for now. It will, of course, be reformed the next time around.

So, is that the end of this tale?

We have described to you that we stumbled across this galaxy sized atom floating in nothingness, discovered that it was a kind of giant womb for all the aspects of life that would be necessary to create all the myriad aspects of creation and these aspects of life were given life through the simple process of using the Law of Mutual Attraction to draw weak gravity together and that gravity was caused to vibrate at a certain, unique frequency and that created life.

Then this life grew because all that exists is consciousness and the more anything can realize and absorb that consciousness the more it grows in terms of life force just like an embryo in a mother's womb.

Eventually, when all the life forces have reached a certain level they were transferred to the 8th dimension of our existence and the womb creation dissolved back into néant.

That, in a nutshell is the process of the creation of basic life, but is it really the end of the story, the end of this book?

It seems to us that there are still a number of unanswered questions and that perhaps, with the help of our Archangelic mentors we can still fill in a few of the gaps.

CHAPTER 8

UNRAVELLING THE MYSTERIES

We came across a number of points as we were investigating this womb like galaxy in which primitive life was formed and we also saw a number of points of connection to life as we know it in what we call our reality. So, although we have done our best to describe what we observed and understood concerning the creation of life, we could end the book here, but as it is fairly short, we thought that we would take a few pages discussing other, but related, aspects of life not, perhaps, directly connected to the subject under discussion but of interest to those wishing to have as complete a knowledge of esoteric matters as possible.

You may consider this section as a sort of addendum rather like we added at the end of book 3.
It is our opinion that as all life is connected and, ultimately, one, to consider any aspect of it in isolation inevitably leaves gaps because one can usually find threads enabling the disparate elements to be linked to the whole.
One, perhaps not very good example would be a set of chess pieces.
Each piece moves independently but, together, they create a collective that moves almost as one piece.

The first aspect of what we studied in this womb like place made us see a possible connection to the development of life as we see it in our reality.
For example, by an almost alchemical means, the joining of male and female DNA enables life to be formed. Of course, we know that the actual life essence has been created as we explained in the main part of the book.
But from then on, on Earth, whether the life force is connected to an egg; chicken, lizard or fish, or, indeed, develops in the womb of a mammal; human or animal, the process develops on similar lines. The tiny life force develops in a protective cocoon. This might be an eggshell or it might be a womb in the case of a mammal.
So, we can see a direct link to this galaxy sized kindergarten or rather the molecule within the kindergarten.
We saw a protective shell of strong gravity with a mass of weak gravity inside that permitted the life force to grow to a certain point at which point it is transferred to another aspect for its development and we might say that it is born.

Of course, we see exactly the same process with life on Earth.
The embryo develops, either in a shell or in a womb until it is ready to take the next step, and then it is born.

We must at all times remember that what we are observing in both cases are different aspects of the same life forces.
In one instance it is all happening in high aspects of the astral spheres and in the other it is occurring on what we consider to be the Earth, terra firma.

But they are both aspects of the same life forces.

What is interesting is that there appears to be two births.
In one case life is created and nurtured to a certain point where it is still very underdeveloped but sufficiently mature as to be able to survive outside of its kindergarten womb and continue its long journey through the dimensions and, in the second, it continues from a protective but "physical" womb or shell and breaks free to grow in a physical universe.

But, if we think calmly about it we see that the two processes are closely linked, one being the creation of life without which the body could not live, and the second, the body, without which incarnation could not happen and would make physical life impossible.

So, the two are just different faces of the same coin.

You may have wondered, as you started to read the first pages of this book, why we chose to present it to you at this point and what possible connection it could have to the previous books that we presented, but we hope that you can now see that it is very relevant information and ties in very nicely to the last book about Auras.
As we have previously said, we think carefully about what we are going to tell you and in what order we should present any information and it seemed to us that this was the moment to present to you information about the beginnings of life.

We have been asked to make it clear to you also that the books we dictate to you are the same books that are read by students of the esoteric in the heavenly spheres.
We have previously explained that once your incarnation on Earth is finished and you return home to the higher 4th dimension, where we all live, you have total freedom to do whatever you want.
But for those who wish to pursue education in any fashion we have a large number of schools where any subject imaginable can be studied – provided that it is not evil or harmful in any way. We do not encourage people to learn the black arts!

But for those wishing to learn the subjects we teach you, subjects that we might call aspects of the esoteric, there are, in the Akash a large number of books on those subjects and teachers use those books to help students progress in knowledge.
The students are trained to visit the Akashic Record and select and read the large numbers of books available on these subjects, written by wise beings.
You will notice that we spoke of the esoteric in the plural as it is not just one subject. There are many aspects of life and many areas that one can study, many avenues that one can explore.

But we wish you to know that these books that we present to you now are part and parcel of the same books that you could study in heaven and by learning the contents of these books during your incarnation and practicing the exercises we propose; meditation for example, you will be getting a head's start for when your incarnation ends and you return home to the higher 4th dimension.

So, we wish to start this additional part by discussing just what God and the Archangels are as far as we are aware.

We know that we have talked about the creative force that we refer to as God many times before and have even suggested that all that exists is God.

We have suggested to you that God is part and parcel of this force called the Law of Mutual Attraction, and the God force has been instrumental in creating all that is.

All that we told you is, of course, true.

But, now we wish to take a deep look behind the scenes, so to speak, and give you as clear a picture of how we understand that this all important creative force is and enable you clearly to picture just what God is as far as we are aware.

Now, as we start, we must make clear to all who are in the folds of any religion that we do not wish to offend nor destroy faith in God. Quite the contrary.

But we must look at this force we call God in as rational a manner as possible and ignore any preconceived notions as to what God might be.

For too long has God been presented as a vindictive tyrant waiting to cause unceasing suffering to all and to any that do not follow a particular religion and to bow on bended knee begging forgiveness and favor.

This is not how we see God at all.

So, let us begin to try to understand what God is and to clarify any preconceived notions concerning him.

Perhaps we should start by repeating what we have already said concerning the English languages and its shortcomings in terms of some explanations of concepts.

We have, in the English language, three words that can be used to describe something; he, she or it. That is all.

He describes a male, she describes a female and it describes something without gender.

Those three words are usually sufficient to describe everyday objects but fail when trying to describe God.

The Bible usually calls God "he", but why should God be male? What proof does anyone have that God is male?

Equally, should we call God "she", it doesn't seem to fit somehow. To call God "it" might be more accurate but the word "it" seems rather cold and unfeeling and one, somehow, feels that God deserves a better appellation than "it".

So, we have this problem. We do not wish to offend anyone's sensibilities when trying to describe God, but we are of the opinion that God is without gender, neither male nor female, so we can't really use the words he or she with any conviction.

As we just said, to call God "it" might be more accurate, but the word feels a bit dismissive, almost as if we were referring to an object, a table or a chair for example.

We hope that God has greater importance than an inanimate object.

But we have just three words at our disposal; he, she or it.

Now, we will not use the word she in relation to God as that word is not generally used and might cause confusion so, with apologies to any ladies who might be reading this book, we will generally refer to God as "he", with occasional use of the word "it".

Also, we will not give God a capital H, as in He nor a capital I as in It. We will just use he or it.

Having said that, let us begin to try to analyse who or what God is as far as we have been able to ascertain.

As we have said about a number of aspects of life, it is sometime easier to start by describing what something is not, rather than what it is, so that when we have subtracted what a thing is not, what is left must be what is – we hope.

As we have often stated in the past, God is not some tyrannical, revengeful monster sitting on a cloud, surveying you all, hoping to catch you out in some act that he can point a finger at and condemn you to an everlasting hell for his delight.

Nor is he a similar figure who will do much the same if you do not belong to Christianity and accept that Jesus died to save you from your sins.

This strange concept is accepted by so many, but a moment's thought would realize that it is not possible for any one person to sacrifice themselves so that countless millions could live a life of sin in the sure knowledge that they are protected from accountability through a belief in a third party – Jesus.

This actually is rather sad and many, once their incarnations are finished and they enter the heavenly spheres fully expecting to be welcomed into God's arms through a belief that Jesus has in some way absolved them from payment, find themselves, once they have had their life review and in the realisation of their many sins, drawn to a level of hell.

It comes as a shock to many, but life deals in realities, not beliefs, and such people should have had the intelligence to reject false teachings and live a life of Godliness and not of sin, feeling protected by a false teaching.

We will also say that many preachers, priests and pastors who teach these false beliefs similarly find themselves in the dark regions once their incarnations finished, firstly, for their own sins, and secondly for the sin of pushing others to commit sin expecting not to have to pay.

Having explained that Christianity contains some false teachings, we will also say that Islam is also a religion that contains much false teaching.

However, having explained that God is not to be found attached to any religion, let us go on and say that God has little to do with fate.

How many people go to church or mosque and get down on their knees or grovel on the floor begging God to save them from some fate or to provide them with more money or some other item?

God doesn't work like that and we will say that it is rare today to find God's angels assisting at any religious ceremony, whatever version of religion is being practiced.

The powers that work for positivity have long since abandoned such places, which either remain empty or attract unpleasant spirits to them. Sensitive people can recognize the coldness that lack of positive thoughts provoke.

Therefore, we wish to point out a clear difference between the study of God and the study of any religion. Whilst we give anyone the right to belong to any religion, we wish to underline the fact that God is not to be found in churches or mosques.

Equally, God would not be found in any mathematical formula.
Science or scientists are often atheists, and one can understand that, as even a lifetime of studying science would not reveal God, as God is only vaguely to be found in the study of living creatures and not at all in mathematics.
But at the same time, we must recognize that God is responsible for the creation of everything and thus whatever we look at in what is called reality is created by God.

What makes it so difficult is that when we observe something "physical", we are looking at the end result whereas God is the prime cause – the opposite end of the chain.
Therefore, to find God we need to climb the mountain of life to the summit and look from that vantage point and, perhaps, we might find a trace of what we seek – God.

So, having spoken briefly of what God is not, let us try to make a list of what we know God is.

We know that God always works with Archangels who implement his plans.
Thus, we assume that God cannot directly create anything but relies on his lieutenants, the Archangels, to carry out his orders and put into manifestation God's concepts.

So, it is no good looking directly at any object, no matter in what dimension it might be found, because there is at least one step between God and the object. Everything was made by Archangels or lesser entities working to implement God's instructions so whatever we observe might well hold the marks of Angelic intervention but would contain no trace of God himself.

But, at the same time, when we look at what we refer to as life, we clearly see the trace of some mastermind who worked and is working behind the scenes to create all this wonder.

Therefore, to find God, we need to take steps into the unknown and, perhaps, the unknowable.

The trouble is where to start?
We are sure that there is some master force, some master mind that exists that is responsible for the creation of what we can only term "life" or "existence".
Equally we are sure that this force does not have physical or astral form. It may well be responsible for designing physical or astral objects but is not itself physical nor astral.
Then we know that God has no gender, male/female, nor does he (it), God, have any sense of race or color. God might be responsible for creating beings with different skin

colors, but is not, himself, the least bit concerned with the problems this has caused over the years.

Further, no matter how far we travel back in time, nor out into the galaxy, no matter how much we delve into the mysteries of life in all respects, we can never find God.
So, we question if God really exists?
Could there be an explanation of life coming into existence that could preclude prime creator?
But the conundrum would be that if we could find where life came from – not just the life that we mentioned before, but the whole complex paraphernalia that exists – would not the force that created it all be God?

So, as we so often do when we are stuck for an answer, we contact the human Archangels that not only have a vast treasure house of knowledge, but have access to the restricted section of the Akashic Record.

The Archangels tell us that this prime creative force both exists and does not exist.
Let us explain by going back to the onion that we mentioned before and that we pulled to pieces in our attempt to find the "God particle" that created the onion.
You may remember that we failed to find anything beyond the many slices, layers of onion.
But we know that, before we cut it to pieces, the onion was alive and had grown from a seed into this very useful vegetable.

So, we can start to understand what the Archangels were trying to tell us.
If we rip the onion to piece, in effect, the life force we call God withdraws and the onion parts die.
But, when it was whole, it contained the life force we call God.

Now, we realize that we have over simplified the concept of life and death, of God and not God, but we wish you to comprehend that, for God really to be in association with something, that something must be in a position to benefit from the life force.
If it is mutilated, as we did to the onion by peeling the layers off, the God spirit withdraws.

It is the completeness of the object that attracts the force we call God or could we say that because the God force is there, an object can be formed.

So, does this give us any indication of what God is?

We can say that when the concept of an object is formed, something we call God takes charge of that object, gives it "life" and the object grows to fulfil its function, whatever that might be.

However, as usual, we have described the effect of God in an object but have not described God itself... or have we?

66

To cut a long story short once again, we can tell you, if you are prepared to believe, that God is the desire, the consciousness, of any and of all objects, whatever they might be, animal, vegetable or mineral, to be created.

This is a complicated concept and we would like to expand on this statement and try to make it more comprehensible.

We have stated that all that really exists is this strange idea "consciousness". Nothing else actually exists and yet through consciousness we have, apparently, all the world that surrounds us, past, present and future, in all the dimensions including all the various life forms that are known as aliens.

This vast complexity of life is all created by desire of one sort or another and it comes from consciousness.

So, we can say that all that exists is consciousness.

Therefore, if all that exists is consciousness, it follows that if something we refer to as God exists, God is consciousness.

As we have stated before, it may be difficult for those who have been brought up to think of God as a person to realize that God is consciousness, nevertheless, it is important for the development of mankind to dispel myths and to base our thinking on reality, as far as we are able.

Consciousness, of course is both single and multiple. There is only one consciousness for all life but, at the same time it is obvious that everyone and everything is conscious.

Thus, like so many aspects of life we have these two effects, single and plural.

We mentioned earlier that the Archangels created primitive life through making gravity vibrate within a sphere but also, so that that life form could develop also endowed that life force with curiosity, which is another way of describing consciousness.

Thus, as these life forms develop it is thanks to this consciousness that creates the desire to so develop.

If it were not for this curiosity to discover aspects of life, all life forms would remain in the same primitive state as when they were first created.

So, what can we make of all this in relation to this being we refer to as God, the all that is, existence, our Father?

God, it appears, is actually the creation born from everyone's individual and collective consciousness, created in conjunction with curiosity.

Now, we realize that this explanation is a bit feeble as if we have missed some important aspect of life and that God is far greater than that. But we must never underestimate the power and scope of consciousness.

If we could peel away all the layers of life in all dimension and in every area of creation, all that would be left is this invisible, indestructible force we call consciousness, universal, cosmic consciousness.

But of course, it begs the question of just where this consciousness came from?

We have mentioned the Archangels who are actually the creative force that work for God, putting God's plans and desire into action.

Where did they come from?

The answer appears to be that they were formed also from consciousness by taking a different route to humanity but, at the expense of disappointing people deeply interested in this subject, there are aspects of consciousness that are too complicated to explain at the moment and so we will not discuss this matter further for the moment.

We have answered the question of who or what God is and we must leave further investigation until mankind is a little more developed.

The next topic that we wish to investigate a little further is life itself.

We have already explained as clearly as we can that every molecule was created in the nursery that we investigated - aided by our human Archangels who so ably advised us and without whom much of this book, and others, could not have been produced. We are greatly indebted to these noble beings for disturbing the bliss of their high planes and of descending to our level to impart their wisdom to us enabling us to reveal to you the information that has been kept from mankind for long ages. We hope that you, too, will take a moment to send your thoughts of gratitude to them.

It is also thanks to these Archangels that we can expand on the concept of life.

Now, we stated that primitive life was created in this nursery and that life was given consciousness that we might also refer to as curiosity. All life has a certain amount of curiosity.

So, curiosity in conjunction with consciousness causes things to want to explore, to start to think, to experiment and so, gradually these primitive life forms develop a greater awareness that they are conscious.

Thus, life, curiosity and consciousness are all combined and we can say that they are one.

To explain this statement, if something is not alive, it cannot be conscious.

We break off here for a moment to discuss A.I., artificial intelligence.

There have been developed recently what have been called supercomputers. Now, these are still fairly primitive compared to some computers created by some alien groups for various reasons; data collection and influencing mankind being just two reasons.

The supercomputers created by Earth scientists are mainly used for data collection and are fairly harmless, but those more advanced alien ones can be used to harm people and are a source of great worry.

However, even the most advanced computers, for the moment, can only think according to their programming and thus are very limited and cannot really be called alive, although some of them can ape life quite well. But even the most advanced alien computer could be revealed as to its limitations if asked a question outside of its programming.

So, A.I. is not life.

Life, for it to be called life, must have independent curiosity about life and to be also linked to collective consciousness in order to maintain the link to the oneness of life.

No A.I. machine can ever be human in that sense.

68

A.I., when very advanced can be programmed to imitate human emotions but it remains just a machine, programmed to imitate humans. But it is surprising the number of humans that can be fooled by alien A.I. into thinking that they are in contact with a human from another dimension. This is a danger we would like exposed.

But to return to life. To be alive is to have some curiosity about life.
Now, we have said that even a grain of sand is alive, but can it have curiosity? Why not? Who amongst you can say what the limitations of a grain of sand are and if it teaches you to be a more considerate person towards all things, it will help you advance towards this so-called ascension.

Therefore, to consider life, it must have a degree of consciousness and a degree of awareness and curiosity no matter how inert a life form might appear.

In the case of humans, we are sorry to say that many are still stuck in the primitive stages, caring only for themselves, being easily swayed by basic emotions, hate, jealousy, anger, vindictiveness to name just a few.
No human truly awake would ever consider eating sentient creatures, hurting others physically or mentally, going to war – whatever the cause – or causing harm to anyone or anything.

To be alive is to realize that all is one and any negative act to anything is to cause harm to oneself.
Love, compassion, understanding, help and giving are the attributes that consciousness should guide one to.
That which a person wishes for himself, he must give out to others because those others are himself.
There is, in fact, no separation in life because all the people who have lived, are living or will live are just aspects of one consciousness, an illusion created by everyone's curiosity to learn about life.

So, there is only one life and that life, if we strip away the layers as if peeling an onion, ultimately, we see that is consciousness.
Life is consciousness and consciousness is one, so all life is one.
You are everyone and everything, and all those things are you.
It is a lesson worth learning.

We will end this book here and allow you to digest all the information it contains.

Printed in Great Britain
by Amazon

80247567R00041